MEDITATION Q & A

Meditation
Q & A

Questions submitted to online forums,
answered by

Prahas

Esmerelda Publishing Company

FIRST EDITION

Designer: Prahas

Dedication

This work is dedicated to those who:

* touch my heart;
* receive my gifts;
* heal my wounds;
* look over me with patience and love while I grow up;
* sit in silence with me.

You know who you are.

The small tome is also dedicated to Mom, whose first and strongest impulse is always towards family and a mother's nurturing: thank you for your "above-and-beyond" support.

Further dedications are extended to my stepfather, Martin "Buddha" Moskof, who egged me on when my creative resolve flagged.

The transformers who worked with me for nine years in our school of meditation will undoubtedly recognize their words and ideas in my writings. I am forever grateful to each of them, and I hope with this volume I have played a role in breathing life into their teachings.

At the highest level,
this work is dedicated to my
Beloved Master,
Osho.

Love.

Acknowledgements

Many thanks to the hundreds of meditators, new and practiced, who asked their questions in a corner of cyberspace where I could find them and reflect on them and respond to them.

These unknown angels gave me a gift of immense size: the opportunity to allow words describing love and meditation to flow out of the body-mind-Being named Prahas towards other human beings.

This flowing created warmth for me during some of the coldest mornings I have experienced.

So thank you, one and all!

Introduction

One morning in early 2010 an idea came to me. At that time, I had been practicing meditation for 17 years. I had been a full-time student in a school of meditation for nine of those years. And I had spent six of those years in near-total solitude.

I had been reading about question and answer web sites on the Internet: places where people from all over the world go to post their questions on any subject and where others go to answer them. I thought, "why not go online and see if people are asking about meditation?"

Sure enough, they were.

Twenty one months later I had answered close to 400 questions. Most of them address questions which 'newbies' (beginners to meditation) have posted. A few delve into deeper waters.

One thing I discovered as I roamed the Q&A forums is there are many people out there who have heard of or read about meditation, and who are trying it out on their own. Many are trying various techniques with no support from experienced practitioners, and some are getting into trouble. An example:

"Kundalini meditation really messed me up. THIS MEDITATION IS THE REAL DEAL AND NOW I HAVE ALL THIS STRESS AND ANXIETY BECAUSE OF IT. WHAT DO I DO NOW?"

One goal of this book is to provide grounded guidance to those meditators experimenting in the privacy of their homes.

My master (guide into the intricacies of meditation) defined a clear distinction between a master and a teacher. A master is one who can help transform a disciple as he progresses along the pathless path of meditation. A teacher may be able to speak about what will happen, but she is incapable of assisting in the transformation. If a teacher can describe in words a beautiful mountain trail, and some of the sights one will see along the way, a master can function as a mountain guide, walking alongside the hiker as he makes the arduous ascent to the summit.

I am not a master. I am a teacher. As a new student sits on the river's edge, dangling his feet into the water, testing its temperature, I can alert him to what he will experience when he learns to swim. When he leaves the river's shore, wades into the water and finally allows the current to take him, he then will be ready for a master.

And in keeping with the tradition of the great masters down through the ages, when the student is ready, the master will appear, prepared to assist in the transformations from student to disciple, from disciple to devotee, and from devotee to enlightened one.

Some of the answers have "Questioner's Comments" after them. One of the web sites I worked on allowed the questioner to choose a best answer (from among all of the answers posted), and then to comment on it. It is this comment that is re-printed here.

I have taken the liberty of editing answers which, upon re-reading, did not do the question justice. The questions have been reprinted verbatim.

All web citations within were active links as of September 1, 2011.

Table of Contents

Speak of Love's Glory?
How do you dare?
I gave my mouth to God
To do with what was wanted;
For years, it was buried
At the bottom of the sea;
Today it is birthed,
Brimmed with living pearls.[1]

0 - Two Meditation Techniques Mentioned Throughout the Book

"'Love yourself,' says Buddha. And then immediately he adds, 'and watch.' The first requirement is to love yourself, and then watch. If you don't love yourself and start watching, you may feel like committing suicide.

"Many Buddhists feel like committing suicide because they don't pay attention to the first part of the sutra, they immediately jump to the second: watch yourself. In fact, I have never come across a single commentary on The Dhammapada, on these sutras of the Buddha, which has paid any attention to the first part: love yourself.

"Socrates says, 'know thyself,' and Buddha says, 'love thyself.' And Buddha is far truer, because unless you love yourself you will never know yourself - knowing comes only later on. Love prepares the ground."[2]

--Osho

Throughout the book, I will be referring questioners to a meditation technique called "gibberish." I will define it here, and simply refer to it by name in the answers below.

In gibberish, you make all kinds of sounds, as long as they are not a real language. Pretend you are talking in a language no one knows. Make loud sounds, soft sounds, angry sounds, sad sounds, just create any non-word sounds you like. Really get into it! And move your body around too.

After five or ten minutes, stop, and sit silently for five minutes, becoming aware of your thoughts, feelings, or sensations. Just watch. Do not try to change or fix anything. Do not try to stop the mind. Love yourself, and accept whatever happens from your heart.

After a month, if you feel to, increase the time for each section by five minutes. Let the new duration settle for a month. Over time, you may end up doing 30 minutes of catharting and 30 minutes of silence.

You may be wondering, "why gibberish?" The enlightened master Osho explains the need for active meditations in the modern world: "In Buddha's time, dynamic methods of meditation were not needed. People were more simple, more authentic. They lived a more real life. Now, people are living a very repressed life, a very unreal life. ... Many incomplete experiences go on being collected, piled up inside their minds.

"Just sitting directly in silence won't help. The moment you will sit silently, you will see all sorts of things moving inside you. ... First throw those things out. ... All the dynamic meditations are preparatory to real meditation. They are just basic requirements to be fulfilled so that meditation can happen."[3]

Another technique referred to below is vipassana meditation. According to Wikipedia, "Vipassana is one of the world's most ancient techniques of sitting meditation, the inception of which is attributed to Gautama Buddha." For the silent section of gibberish, the meditator might choose to do this technique.

Vipassana involves watching the breath. You simply sit comfortably, perhaps with legs crossed, always with back straight, and you watch as the breath comes into your belly and leaves your belly. No alteration of the breathing is needed. Your eyes may remain closed or half-open. If your awareness leaves your breath (as it almost certainly will!), simply notice, "ah, I am not watching my breath," and bring your attention back to your breath. Do not try to stop your mind, or change or fix anything. Simply watch with non-judgment -- whatever is, is alright. Witness the thoughts, feelings, and sensations without being for nor against them. Observe them the way a scientist might observe an experiment. Accept them from your heart.

Begin with five or ten minutes a day, in the morning or around sunset. After a month, increase the time if it feels right to do so.

The Q-and-A

1 - The Basics

You must take meditation as a game, a child's game. People who meditate should be playful –playing with existence, playing with life – weightless, non-tense; not in a doing mood but in a relaxed mood. It is only in a relaxed moment, only in a playful moment, that the happening is possible.[4]

--Osho

Q.
What is meditation?

A.
Meditation is the path to enlightenment. One begins by choosing a meditation technique, which helps one to become more aware of one's thoughts, feelings, and physical sensations. Over time, one's awareness grows, and one becomes conscious of deeper and deeper levels of one's being. Finally, the dew drop of the individual "I" drops into the ocean of cosmic consciousness, and enlightenment is attained.

Put another way, meditation leads to the understanding that you are not the mind, you are not the feelings, and you are not the body: in fact, *you* are not. There is only pure awareness, pure consciousness.

[Author's Note: These words -- awareness, consciousness, enlightenment -- are problematic, because they describe phenomena which are very difficult to put into language. While I expand on them in other answers in the

book, the reader will need to settle for a vague sense of the meaning of these words until she begins her practice of meditation, and starts to taste for herself the true definitions, which reside beyond thoughts and words.]

There are many different meditation techniques, but all of them have one thing in common: they all cause you to become more self-aware and more watchful of your inner world.

Some techniques are still: for example, you sit and watch your breath. Others are active, asking you to move, dance, make sounds, etc.

Perhaps the best thing to do is look around at different techniques and find one which "feels right." Then go ahead and try it for a few weeks.

Q.
Why meditate?

A.
Many people begin to meditate because a gentle longing arises in them -- a longing to know the answer to a few basic questions: who am I? Is there something beyond the three-dimensional world? What is life ultimately about?

This longing propels a person into meditation, because masters from all traditions down through the ages have promised that if you meditate, you will begin to get a glimpse into the answers to these questions.

Q.
What are the benefits of meditation?

A.

Meditation may strengthen awareness. Meditation may bring a sense of calm. Meditation may help us to see that fulfilling the desires of the mind will not bring a lasting sense of contentment.

And all of these things change the way we act in our everyday lives. When a business deal falls through, we do not take it as hard. When someone cuts us off on the highway, we laugh instead of yell. When we have an hour between appointments, we stop and breathe into our bellies and enjoy simply being, rather than playing video games.

Q.

I'm interested in meditation. Where is a good place to start getting information about it?

A.

The best thing, in my opinion, is to look around your physical location for groups who meditate, or do yoga, tai chi, or other meditative practices. Then go and sit in on the classes (as an observer). You may find that each has its own unique flavor, and one will resonate with you more than the others. Trust your heart and intuition. Much more can happen if you work with a group, than if you are on your own.

Q.

Can someone give me a good meditation reflection or reading to start my day?

A.

Why read about meditation when you can meditate? Would you ask a thirsty person to sit and look at a glass of water, or would you invite them to drink? Why not begin with a meditation technique called gibberish?[5]

Q.

What is the difference between meditating and cogitating?

A.

My dictionary defines cogitate as follows: "think deeply about something." Meditation has *nothing* to do with thinking. Meditation is about awareness, about that which resides beyond mind, beyond thought, and beyond feeling. So please, do not confuse meditating with cogitating.

Q.

Does meditation change the way your brain works? I've heard that people who meditate often spontaneously go into trance-like states. The spontaneity of it seems like there's an actual biological change occurring in the brain. Is this true?

A.

There are many studies showing various changes in the brain which result from meditation. Regardless, the main thing is to keep practicing![6]

Q.

Does meditation have anything to do with god and religion?

A.

If you are unsure about the existence of god, you are beginning in the perfect state of mind.

In Zen, they talk about "don't know" mind. Whenever you are asked a question (What is love? Is there a god?) you think, "I don't know." This keeps your mind open to new experiences.

My suggestion is you find a meditation technique that feels right, and dive in! Notice your thoughts, feelings, and physical sensations. Do not try to stop the mind. Just love yourself and watch.

Over time, many things about yourself and the universe will be revealed.

Q.
Are the effects of meditation gradual or immediate?

A.
While you may feel certain changes for a few hours here and there early on in the process, for the effects to become integrated time is required.

And yet -- the present is here now, available in this very moment. No waiting is needed.

The challenge is this: the mind has been chattering away for a long time, and it may take a while for the awareness to become strong, so that you can stay in the here-and-now.

Q.
Will mind-wandering during meditation lower the benefits?

A.
No. The mind will wander during meditation. Simply notice it, without judging or feeling bad, and return to practicing the technique with which you are working.

Q.
Is it possible to meditate too much? I have a lot of stress as well as a lot of trouble concentrating and I was wondering if it's ok to meditate for an hour or more, daily. Do any complications or issues arise when meditating for too long or too frequently?

A.
It depends on many things. If you are just starting out, five or ten minutes a day would be fine. As you go deeper, you will likely want to do more.

On retreats, people meditate for six - eight - ten hours a day. In most cases, people vary the techniques they do throughout the day. And when meditating this much, it is good to be with a teacher, guide or master.

During a regular work day, after you've gained experience, probably an hour a day is about right.

But again, it depends on many factors, and on who you are. Let your feelings be your guide. If it feels right, continue. If you start to feel off, slow down and do less. Don't let your mind force you into more than feels good. (But also don't let your mind tell you to stop!)

Q.
What psychological value is there in meditation?

A.
The basic thing to be understood is this: meditation teaches you to watch your mind. Meditation teaches you there is such a thing as awareness, which resides *beyond* the mind. When you bring awareness to each moment, you can witness thoughts, feelings, emotions, and physical sensations.

Psychology works within the mind and emotions. You sort out thoughts, memories, feelings, and so forth (all of which are mind stuff). This can be useful as a start to get to know yourself.

But in the East, they have known for centuries that this is not enough. To attain to authentic health, one has to go beyond mind. One has to see for oneself that one is not the mind: rather, one is the witnessing consciousness beyond mind.

Once a person has a glimpse of this, all of the daily psychological chatter of the mind becomes much less powerful. It doesn't effect you as much. It is like watching a B-rate sitcom on Fox TV. This brings a lightness to the mood, and I find this of great value.

Q.
I literally just began meditation today. I meditated for 20 minutes and afterwards I noticed some pretty good effects. I did feel a little more relaxed and rejuvenated. Since it was my first time ever, I'm only assuming the effects will go up from here.

A.
You will have "good" days and "bad" days meditating. The important thing is not to get attached to any specific experience. Simply be present, without judging, to whatever is happening.

Q.
I keep attaching myself to thoughts! It's so hard to just see the thought without becoming it. I see it, I try not to try, and I end up trying and failing! It's sooo hard! I'm an extremely obsessive guy and my focus is poor. This makes it even more difficult!

A.
My sense is you need to bring more heartfulness into your practice. Accept whatsoever happens from your heart. The Buddha said, "Love yourself, then watch." Too often meditators forget the first part: love yourself!

If you notice yourself feeling frustrated, then be with frustration. "Hmmm, I'm feeling frustrated. Isn't that interesting?" Frustration is not good or bad, it is just what is happening. If you are greedy for a certain "quiet" experience, notice that. "Hmmm, I want more silence. Interesting. I'm greedy. And I can accept that. I still love myself." Take care!

Q.
Anyone experienced in meditation? I guess you're supposed to observe your thoughts. How exactly do you do that? I either imag-

ine myself looking out a window where my thoughts are going by, or just try to "see" them themselves. How do I know if I'm doing it right though? Because, I kind of listen to a thought and then let it go and listen to the next one. Is that what I'm supposed to do?

A.

If you are working with observing your thoughts, then the last thing you said is closest. Perhaps a better phrase is "mind activity." Observe the thoughts, images and dreams as they pass through the mind. Some people "listen." Some people see images. But as I think, I can notice that I am thinking. It's like, imagine you were going to write a journal -- every thought that passes through your head, write it down. Who would be noticing the thoughts, and writing them down? That is the "observer" part of the mind.

Now -- this is a good first step towards meditation. But it is not the end step. Practice your observing for a month or so, then write me an email and I'll tell you about the next step. Good luck!

Q.
Is taking a dump a form of meditation?

A.
Despite the fact that your question, on its surface, has a certain disrespect in it, I will answer.

Anything you do -- washing the dishes, brushing your teeth, cleaning the floor -- can be a meditation if you do it with awareness. Notice every movement of your hands and arms. Notice the feel of the water on your hands. Notice your breathing as you work.

The more noticing you bring to your body-mind as you do whatever activity you are doing, the more you are moving toward meditation.

Q.
Kundalini meditation really messed me up. THIS MEDITATION
IS THE REAL DEAL AND NOW I HAVE ALL THIS STRESS
AND ANXIETY BECAUSE OF IT. WHAT DO I DO NOW?

A.
Remember the onion analogy? The human psyche is like an onion,
with many many layers. What meditation does is it begins to peel
the top layers off, so you can begin to see other layers that used to
be hidden.

The meditation didn't create the stress and anxiety that you are noticing / feeling. All it did was help you to become aware of what
was already there. No worries -- it is a good sign!

Now comes the part which takes a little courage. Keep going. Do a
little each day (don't over-do the meditation, but don't stop either).
Keep breathing. Allow the feelings to come up.

Dance, sing, move around, talk gibberish in the car, anything to
release the stress. And -- you might want to consider finding a
group of people to meditate with -- you don't have to go through it
alone.

Q.
I'm just starting to learn how to meditate, and I want to make sure
that I'm doing this right. Are you supposed to feel tired, drained,
drowsy, heavy, and weak? Thank you!

A.
All kinds of feelings arise when you begin meditating. You are
peeling away the layers of the onion of your personality, and there
will be all kinds of different things. I don't know what technique
you are using, but you may want to try gibberish, to shake some of
the yuckies off.[7]

Q.

Recently I've heard a lot about the benefits of meditation so I decided to try it for myself. However, after a dozen failed attempts to reach any deeper state of consciousness while relaxing my mind and body, I've lost much motivation to try it. I have an extremely active mind.

However, something dawned on me today. I've frequently been to electronic/techno music festivals/events. When I'm there dancing, I find myself to be at my deepest level of consciousness. I move fluently with the music without much effort. I get in tune with the music playing, particularly the beat, and I soon find myself in another level of consciousness. What does this mean?

A.

This is beautiful. My master spoke about the state of meditation which arises when "the dancer becomes the dance;" when "the dancer disappears and only the dance remains."

You might Google "Osho Dynamic Meditation" -- I think you would enjoy!

Q.

I have this dream of wanting the world to be a better place. I don't believe in religion, politics, or therapeutic medication. I want to help people realize themselves through meditation. I love meditating. It helps me and I want to help the world. There is a tour coming up to go across our country and teach. I just started meditating. But I don't know if I should go or not?

A.

In my experience, it takes years and years of practicing meditation before one becomes "qualified" to help others in their search. Patience, my friend. Keep going in, becoming more aware of yourself. The way to help others is to become more meditative yourself.

Q.

What is the difference between prayer and meditation?

A.

There are many different kinds of prayer. Most of them involve some sort of inner dialogue with God. For example, "Please God, grant me serenity..."

Meditation is about strengthening awareness. Awareness is beyond mind, beyond thinking. Yes, thoughts happen. But the meditator watches these thoughts pass, like clouds passing through an open sky.

Occasionally, a person in prayer will be overcome with a tremendous sense of gratitude. This kind of heartful opening-up to divinity is close to meditation, and also occurs beyond mind.

Q.

How do you release bad thoughts and feelings from your mind? What's the best method to release thoughts of anxiety and paranoia out of your mind?

A.

Gibberish meditation.[8]

Q.

I worry a lot and I get depressed a lot because I've just gotten out of a relationship which really hurt me deeply. I need to stop being so stressed out all the time..

A.

Try gibberish meditation.

Q.

What do you think: does the world need medication or meditation?

A.
Meditation is medication. Notice the root of the words is the same.

I heard my master say, there are many diseases, but I prescribe only one treatment: meditation. That being said, there is a place for medication (we are, after all, biochemical organisms).

So I would say -- more meditation, less medication. Let us find a new balance.

Q.
Are there any dangers in meditation? I recently started meditating, and I found my own way of breathing, but then I get to a point where I am hardly breathing.

A.
The most important thing is that you listen to your body. If anything feels odd or uncomfortable, stop meditating for a few days.

Also, I get the sense it might be right for you to work with a group of people. See if there is a group of meditators around. Or if not, maybe a tai chi or yoga class. Visit a few groups and sign up with the one that feels right.

Q.
What are proven ways to unlock the subconscious? I'm starting to realize how I am constantly sabotaging myself through my subconscious. I really want to resolve that once and for all. I've done therapy etc, even did primal for a while and that didn't lead to much. Would anyone have a suggestion - might meditation be useful?

A.
Meditation is all about looking in, and discovering what resides in the inner world. You will first encounter thoughts, feelings, and physical sensations which you are likely familiar with. Over time, your "flashlight" of awareness will grow stronger, and you will

begin to penetrate the unconscious. In my opinion, meditation is the best possible thing for you to attain what you seek.

Q.
How to remove negative thoughts instantly & become free and happy?

A.
It is completely impossible. Meditation is about accepting, from your heart, what is. Then, if negative thoughts happen, no problem! You accept them from your heart.

Q.
What is the purpose of the specific posture during meditation? When I have meditated, the specific posture called for seemed very rigid & stiff to me. In fact, it caused both myself & the person who I meditated with to get horrific headaches & backaches. Has anyone else experienced this?

A.
Be comfortable! Love your body! The main thing is to keep your back straight. If you can sit cross legged, and use pillows to make yourself comfy and keep your back straight, good. Otherwise, sit in a straight back chair.

Q.
If you play guitar half an hour every day can this be a type of meditation? What if I play metal, but unplugged??

A.
Yes. If you get totally into it, so that you disappear, and only the guitar playing remains, it becomes a meditation technique.

Metal is not the most conducive music to meditation. Why not try something softer? The reason is this: as you meditate, you become more sensitive. You will be able to hear all kinds of nuances in music that is not as harsh as metal. Eventually, even one chord, played softly on a 12-string acoustic, will have so much beauty in it....

Q.
Before I compete I always sit by myself and meditate breathing in and out slowing and calming my self down because I'm always nervous. Are there any other types of mediation that have these same effects or better?

A.
It is good you are remembering to breathe, and that you are noticing a calming effect.

But -- meditation is not designed to help you compete more effectively. Meditation helps you become more aware of what is, in this moment, without changing or fixing anything. If you notice you are feeling lazy, you simply notice it. You don't try to change it. If you notice you are feeling "pumped up," notice that too.

So -- if competing is your primary focus, you may not be ready for meditation just yet.

Q.
Does meditation really work? Look, sometimes I get nervous for no reason, and I want to solve this problem without any kind of medication. Does meditation really help for nerves and anxiety?

A.
There are many causes of anxiety in today's world. The easy fix is to take a pill. The more real (and more costly) solution is to go deep into yourself to see what is making you tick.

If you are ready to invest in yourself, and in Truth, then begin meditation. In general, you probably want to look for techniques that move the body, rather than stationary techniques. This will help you throw off some of the nervous energy.

Q.
Is Buddhism the best way to enlightenment and spirituality? If Buddhism is your path to enlightenment, what are the books you recommend? And can meditation effect dreams, habits, or even personality?

A.
Have a look at "Cutting Through Spiritual Materialism," by Chogyam Trungpa. The real deal.

It is *meditation* that will grow your awareness and prepare you for enlightenment. What makes a particular strain of Buddhism powerful is its emphasis on meditation.

Yes -- meditation will effect the things you mention. In fact, the entire purpose of meditation is to *dissolve* your personality, so that you can come to know something more precious: your Being.

Don't get caught up in reading. Pick a technique that feels right, and jump in. It is the most incredible journey you will ever take.

2 - Advanced Basics

"[The awakened one] is aware of what is going on in the present moment, what is going on in his body, feelings, mind and objects of mind. He knows how to look deeply at things in the present moment. He does not pursue the past nor lose himself in the future, because the past is no longer and the future has not yet come. If we lose the present moment, we lose life."[9]

--Buddha

Q.

Can you know divinity through meditation?

A.

It is a beautiful question. If you choose a meditation technique (for example, watching your breath), the awareness will begin to get stronger. First, the ability to notice thoughts, feelings, and physical sensations will improve. Then, over time, if all of the masters down through the ages are correct (and I can add my own experience as well), you will begin to notice a certain beauty, blissfulness, benediction. And not only inside of yourself: but also, radiating out from the trees, the rocks, the stars. This, to me, is the beginning of knowing divinity.

Q.

Why can Buddhists and Jews and Wiccans and other religionists share similar meditative practices?

A.

All meditation techniques share one thing in common: they all emphasize the growth of awareness. They bring one's attention to the witnessing consciousness which lies beyond mind, feeling, and body.

Because meditation is concerned with that which lies beyond mind (and therefore ideas, thoughts, and ideologies) it can be used by anyone with any set of beliefs. A Buddhist can watch her thoughts about Buddhism float through the mind. A Jew can notice his thoughts about the Old Testament. A Wiccan can sit silently, unmoving, as thoughts of the solstice pass through.

Meditation teaches that *all* of these thoughts are simply mind-stuff. The light of awareness lies beyond them. And, this light is the *same* light for each of us. Thus all of the great masters have proclaimed, "we are one."

Q.
Which yoga or meditation is good for increasing will-power?

A.
None of them. The whole purpose of meditation and yoga is to help you to *dissolve* your will power. When you meditate, you begin to see that all desire leads to suffering. This means that all of your greed, ambition, lust, and so forth contribute to your suffering. They get in the way of you connecting to godliness. They clog you up, so you cannot be available to the divinity which stands ready to stream forth into your being.

Will power, as it is normally understood, is *you* wanting to do something. To achieve something. The whole purpose of meditation is to dissolve this desiring mind, this ambitious mind. And ultimately, to dissolve this "you" that you are so attached to.

So please, if you are seeking to increase your will-power, do not start yoga or meditation.

Q.
How do I meditate without falling asleep every time? I have guided meditation recordings. I know that I'm supposed to be in

that 'twilight' state of mind but I can't seem to stay there. I like to meditate before going to sleep every night.

A.

I would suggest meditating in the morning, before you eat. Another suggestion: before you start, spend five minutes doing gibberish.[10] Then do your regular technique.

You are not supposed to be in a 'twilight' state, or any other state. You are simply to notice what is in the moment. Do not try to change or fix anything. When things change, as they will, do not try to "stay" in one state. Just watch as things change. And if you try to stay in one state, watch that. "Hmm, some part of my mind is attempting to preserve my current state of consciousness. Interesting."

If you still have trouble falling asleep (in the morning), have a cup of green tea before you start.

Questioner's Comment:
Twilight is the state where you reach your subconscious mind, my goal in meditation.

Q.
How can I hallucinate during meditation?

A.
Why would you want to hallucinate during meditation? Meditation is all about cutting through the nonsense, and seeing what is real. You are starting off on the wrong foot. Have a look inside, and see what it is that is motivating you to meditate.

Q.
I'm fairly new to meditation. They talk about there being a certain point where you can be present enough to "watch" your thoughts in

order to dissolve them. How do you tell the difference between thinking them and watching them?

A.
If you notice your thoughts (i.e., if you are able to write down your thoughts in a journal as they appear in your head) then you are perceiving parts of the mind with the observer part of the mind. This is where most meditators begin. Over time, you will become able to observe feelings and physical sensations as well. As more time passes, the observing will shift to "awareness" -- a gentle cloud of knowing which witnesses all that is happening in the body-mind -- a cloud which resides beyond the mind.

Q.
What is the purpose of yoga in real meditation? There are lots of different types of yoga and lots of different types of meditation: some are good, some are better and many are misunderstood. One question I've come back to many times recently is, "what is the primary purpose of yoga, assuming you are learning it for meditation and not physical flexibility." If anyone could send me a good technically detailed answer it would be extremely appreciated!

A.
The primary purpose of yoga is to open up the various energy channels in the body, so that more energy can flow. The more energy flowing, the deeper and more profound the meditation becomes. In the end, meditation is simply about cleaning the rust out of the pipes.

A plumber's technical answer... ;-)

Q.
Can you smoke some good weed and then close your eyes to enhance meditation?

A.

It's not that weed is bad, and I don't care if you do it or not. But it is not going to help your meditation. You may have an "experience" once in a while, but it will quickly fade as soon as the drug wears off. When you practice meditation, the awareness is strengthened, so you can stay "high on life" all day long, without the costs of drugs!!!

Q.

I don't know what is wrong with me. Meditation has been very good for me and I have improved spiritually with meditating. For some reason unknown to me I will stop meditating and praying sometimes just because I get bored of it. Any suggestions to keep going?

A.

The mind will do anything it can to get you to stop meditating, because meditation directs energy away from the mind, and allows it to pool in consciousness. You need to simply decide you are going to continue meditating, and then ignore whatever excuses the mind comes up with to stop. Nothing is wrong with you. The mind is just doing its thing, trying to stay in control. One last point: if you notice an ambitious part of the mind trying to improve spiritually, accept it from your heart, and remember that ambition is just another part of the ego-mind.

Q.

Isn't sleeping another form of meditation?

A.

In sleep one becomes unaware. Thoughts happen, dreams happen, images pass through the mind, but there is no awareness of these things. When meditating, these things happen, but there is a witness, a watcher on the hill: there is awareness of what is happening in the body-mind.

Q.

How long does it take to see the benefits of meditation? I've been meditating for 20 minutes, twice a day, for about a month. I still can't see any positive internal changes. Would living in an abusive/ negative environment prevent these changes from occurring? When I meditate I'm usually calm and peaceful, but I don't feel that way during the day. Please provide some insight. Thank you.

A.

It is very good you have committed to a daily practice. Now, a little patience is needed. The river of your body-mind-Being is muddy, from years of neglect. It may take a little time for the mud to settle, so that clear, fresh water is known and tasted.

If you are living in an abusive / negative environment now, this will add a bit of challenge to things. As you move through this environment, notice how you respond to each event. Over time, you may find more options available to you than you currently see.

If you are talking about a past environment, we all have our histories to deal with. Continue meditating, and all will be revealed and healed in due course.

Questioner's Comment: Thanks for your advice. The abusive / negative environment is actually my home, but leaving isn't really an option at this stage. I will continue to search inside myself, hopefully everything will work out.

Q.

What type of meditation is best for me? I'm very spiritual. I want to have a spiritual experience (an epiphany, imagining a vivid setting, etc.) I'm not really looking to just relax myself, but I'm trying to have an experience.

A.

It is good that you are interested in things beyond the mundane, every day world. But there are a few things to consider as you get started on the path.

The Buddha has said that desire is the root of all suffering. Also, to attain to great heights of consciousness, one needs to see deeply into, and thereby dissolve, all desire.

Now -- desire takes many forms. One can be ambitious for power. One can be greedy for money. One can lust after women. And so forth.

Meditation -- no matter which technique you choose -- is all about becoming present to *what is* in this moment. If you see greed come up, you are present to greed. If you see lust come up, you are present to lust. It is this very presence, this awareness, which be-gins to melt the desire, leaving you lighter, fresher, more loving, more compassionate -- in short, more spiritual.

So please -- when you notice the thought where you are "wanting to have a spiritual experience," be alert! Be present to the thought, rather than acting on the desire. Bring a heartful curiosity to your inner world -- "hmm, I wonder what is going on inside of me? I am simply going to watch, without judging or trying to change or fix anything. I am going to love myself, then watch."

Questioner's Comment: wow... that was deep.

Q.

Meditation is hard to do when you actually need to do it. Bud-dhism's key belief is to abolish suffering in oneself. But I find that when I'm suffering the most, I can't bring myself to meditate. It hurts too much to have those thoughts rush to my head. In facing my suffering it's making me suffer too much.

What do I do? I haven't meditated in almost two weeks because of this. One last thing: meditation isn't exactly clearing your mind. It's just letting the thoughts pass by without controlling them.

A.
The first thing: Buddha did not *believe* it was possible to abolish suffering. He discovered it was in fact possible because he meditated and he achieved an end to suffering. And he shared with the world this fact: you too can end your suffering if you practice meditation.

I can relate to the challenge of meditating when there is pain present. For me, when there is pain near the surface, I will often distract myself with DVDs or whatever. But if I can just bring myself to the moment, to be present to whatever is there, the possibility of transformation, of release is created. And almost always, the *fear* of the thing is much worse than actually *experiencing* the thing.

So take a deep breath, and bring yourself back to the moment. It is in these moments when beautiful, long lasting changes can happen!

Finally, it is beautiful that you are not trying to clear your mind, and just letting thoughts pass. Right on!!

Questioner's Comment: Thank you very very much. :)

Q.
I have been practicing yoga for a few months and practicing celibacy for two months. Whenever I meditate I feel as if I am intoxicated or as if I am drunk. The feeling is just whao [sic] and I want to be in that bliss but sitting in lotus position for more than 90 minutes is difficult for me. I want to know why I feel when I meditate as if I am drunk???

A.

A few things. The word "drunk" conjures up in me a few different feelings. But the main thing is a dimming of awareness, or a confusion, or a sluggishness of mind. Whatever it is, do not judge it. Simply be present to it. Watch the drunkenness. If you can do this, you are meditating.

Re: celibacy. Where did you get the idea to practice it? My opinion is this: if the mind, because of reading or thinking, enforces celibacy on yourself, it is not healthy. You are simply suppressing your sex energy, which is not helpful.

The original celibates gave up sex because it simply didn't happen for them anymore. After a while (probably after a long period of practicing yoga or meditation) their sex energy "moved up," and didn't express as sexual desire. So they stopped having sex.

This is *vastly* different than *deciding* to stop having sex.

So you decide for yourself what is happening for you -- but if you feel sex energy moving, do not suppress it.

It seems like 90 minutes is a long time to sit for a beginner. Are you doing it every day? If you really feel it is right for you, perhaps stretching beforehand would help. And are you sitting in full lotus, or simply cross-legged? If full lotus, perhaps try cross-legged only. Just make sure your back is straight, and it is not much different.

One more thing -- see if you can watch the desire for bliss. "Hmm, interesting, I am desiring bliss." Because there is one certain way to make sure bliss will not arise -- and that is desiring it.

Of course the trap is this: now you will desire to *stop* the desire for bliss. This is just another desire. So simply watch your desire for bliss. "Interesting -- my mind is greedy for bliss." Do not judge or feel bad. Just take note.

Q.
Does the power of prayer work?

A.
You will receive all kinds of answers to this question. My suggestion is you find out for yourself. And my suggestion is, in order to find out, begin to meditate.

Q.
I can't stand inactivity. What to do? I'm very easily bored and feel so empty when bored. ...

At 14 years of age, I started thinking about death and how boring life is. I start thinking that all I do is gonna end one day. I hate thinking about the future because it seems so hollow.

Purpose drives me. For the last few months, I've been driven by the purpose of learning iPhone Programming. ...

Sometimes when I watch movies, music etc, I think "look at us humans, desperately finding ways to avoid boredom." What's my problem?

A.
It is beautiful, the way you are inquiring into the deeper meaning of life. And your focus on the activity / inactivity duality is right on the mark!!!

Yes, most of us use all kinds of distractions to avoid quiet, inactivity and silence. Because silence leads to looking inward, and the first thing we come upon is the mind!

And guess what? The mind is mostly filled with rubbish! The same old tired thoughts running endlessly around like a tape loop. And it is uncomfortable to discover this. So we go back to our TV and our iPods and so on....

It sounds like you are young, but from your question, it seems like you are ready for meditation.

Meditation will teach you how to become aware of your thoughts, feelings, and physical sensations. The important thing to remember, when you start, is not to judge anything. Simply watch, accepting whatsoever is from your heart. I will suggest a technique. For five minutes, do gibberish.[11]

Q.
Don't you think correct breathing technique can resolve many of our problems? I think because of our sedentary lifestyle we inhale less oxygen and exhale less toxic gases. We are suddenly finding some disorders which were not heard of 100 years back when men and women used to work in fields and were required to do lot of aerobic exercises. In modern days also those who do aerobic exercises find many of the psychosomatic problems reduced. Many Indian meditation techniques give great emphasis on correct breathing techniques. What are your views?

A.
I agree. More attention to breathing, and more self-awareness in general, coupled with a good amount of physical exercise and a healthy diet would bring much health to many people. Health brings more contentment, and contentment means less conflict and problems in the world.

Q.
I meditate and I feel like I'm doing something wrong because I think a lot while meditating. Also, it is said that while meditating time passes very quickly. For me time goes very very slowly. 15

minutes feels like three hours. Any advice or anything at all?
Thank you.

A.
Everyone thinks a lot while meditating!!! The thing is, to simply watch the thoughts float by, like clouds in an empty sky. High level thoughts are no better or worse than low level thoughts. They are all clouds, and have nothing to do with you -- that is, with awareness.

As far as the time thing, that is nothing to worry about. For me, sometimes 15 minutes feels like an hour, other times it flies by.

My main advice is to be more gentle with yourself. Patience, please. And no, you are doing nothing wrong.

Q.
Can you experience the notion of God through meditation?

A.
The beautiful thing about meditation is that it does not rely upon "notions" at all. You simply watch: become more aware of your thoughts, feelings, and physical sensations. Over time, your awareness strengthens, and you become more sensitive. And then, if the masters from all traditions down through the ages are correct (and I can say from my own experience I have glimpses that they are) you will come into contact with divinity, with a godliness, in the trees and the stars and inside of your own Being.

Questioner's Comment: Thank you this really helped me out.

3 - The Desire to Stop or Clear the Mind

"Mind is one of the most beautiful mechanisms. Science has not yet been able to create anything parallel to mind. Mind still remains the masterpiece -- so complicated, so tremendously powerful, with so many potentialities. Watch it! Enjoy it! And don't watch like an enemy, because if you look at the mind like an enemy, you cannot watch. ...

Thinking cannot be stopped. Not that it does not stop, but it cannot be stopped. It stops of its own accord. This distinction has to be understood, otherwise you can go mad chasing your mind. No-mind does not arise by stopping thinking. When the thinking is no more, no-mind is. The very effort to stop will create more anxiety, it will create conflict, it will make you split. You will be in a constant turmoil within. This is not going to help."[12]

--Osho

Q.
How to clear one's mind? That is, how to attain a condition of total blankness -- peace -- something which saints acquire by meditation.

A.
If you notice you are trying to clear the mind, do not try to stop yourself from doing it. Simply be present. 'Interesting. A part of my mind is trying to clear the rest of the mind.' It is loving presence which will dissolve the desire to clear the mind.

I ask you, who would be doing the clearing? It would simply be another part of the mind!

Meditation is all about simply being present to what is, without judgment or expectation. If you notice thoughts, good! You are noticing thoughts, and it is the *noticing* that is the awareness, the meditation.

If you notice feelings or physical sensations, good!

Again, if "you" are pushing thoughts away, who is doing it? It is just another part of the mind, and awareness is beyond the mind. Awareness is like a mirror -- it simply reflects what is in front of it, not trying to change or fix it. If a handsome man walks in front of a mirror, the mirror shows him. If a man with a scar on his face is there, the mirror reflects the scar.

This is how your meditation should be -- simply accept what is.

Watch the mind, calmly, not judging, not trying to change or fix anything. Don't give it any juice. Don't be concerned with it. Pretend it is a TV show -- it has nothing to do with you. Over time, on its own, it will slow down. But you cannot make it slow down.

The reason it is hard work to stop thinking is this: who is it that is trying to stop thinking? There must be another part of the mind which is the "thought police" and she is trying to stop the first part of the mind. So you see, it is mind fighting with mind.

[This is such an important point, I will provide more questions to which I gave more or less the same answer.]

Q.
What steps do you take to rid your mind of thoughts and images?

Q.
Are you supposed to think...or not think? What is the answer? Some people say you're supposed to shut off all thought...others say you're supposed to use it to understand...I'm so confused.

Q.

How to stay away from thoughts and chatter?

Q.

I know this is the central question of meditation, and perhaps far too broad, but does anyone have any strategies for quieting all the thoughts of the busy world while meditating?

Q.

I think meditation is very interesting but whenever I try I just get impatient and just stop trying. How do you quiet your mind and just let yourself into that?

Q.

What is the best way to control the mind during meditation?

Q.

What methods do you use to clear your mind and go into a deep meditation? I tried deep breaths to relax at first, that's all good, then I used to say a mantra on the inhale and exhale. Since that hasn't worked, I abandoned it and tried to just clear my mind on my own. But the more I try, the more my mind resists. Can anyone give me some other methods?

A.

The difficulty is not the technique you are using. The difficulty is that you (that is, your mind) are trying to clear your mind. Trying to clear your mind will *never* work. After all, who is doing the clearing? It is just another part of the mind! The part we could call the "spiritual teacher," who read somewhere that meditation should lead to a quiet mind. Please drop that idea.

Meditation is about accepting, fully, from your heart, whatever is happening in the here and now. If thoughts are happening, great! I will be present to thoughts. If emotions happen, super, I will feel my emotions. Simply witness, accept, breathe, and be present in the now.

Love yourself as you are. Love your mind, even as it goes on and on. This is what mind does. Allow it to do its thing. Just watch, like you are an unconcerned observer, neither for nor against anything that happens. And if a desire for a quiet mind arises, watch that desire.

Questioner's Comment: I chose this one as best answer because as I read it, I was trying to do what you were saying, and I instantly felt more present and more aware of my body, and more alive.. so thank you!

Q.
How to meditate....I get distracted easily........? While I try to observe the breath.....I receive more thoughts and chatter in background of meditations...how to catch them while I'm meditating...plz give some good answers...help me...thanx.

A.
If your awareness leaves your breath (as it almost certainly will!), simply notice, "ah, I am not watching my breath," and bring your attention back to your breath. You don't need to "catch" anything. When you notice you have left your breath, go back to it. Don't feel bad. Be playful. Enjoy the movie of your mind...because in the end, it has nothing to do with "who you are."

4 - Emotions

"The practice I describe of observing your emotions, allowing them to be, for somebody who habitually does not express emotions...it is not usually the best way to try and observe his or her emotions because they may not even know what emotions they are having. They may be so much pushed down... So particularly for those people who have been suppressing emotions, it is very helpful to express the emotions -- if possible without injuring anybody, or yourself. To allow yourself to express emotions, and witness that."[13]

--Eckhart Tolle

Q.
What is the best way to get stored anger out without hurting someone? I'm 15 and I have loads of stored up anger from my earlier childhood years because I was bullied like hell for my shape and weight and plus molested. If I for instance kick a bag a lot then I feel good but get quickly angry again so how do I release the anger without damaging myself for good?

A.
I would suggest two things. One is a martial art, like Aikido or Karate. These are very physical activities, so you can release your stored up energy, but they also teach discipline and self-mastery. Also, they will teach you to protect yourself, and help with your weight issues. The other suggestion is gibberish meditation.[14]

Q.
I get angry at the drop of a hat and because of my temper I've hurt many ppl so close to me..like my mother, my bf my best friends etc. I use really abusive words and the minute I calm down I feel soo guilty and apologize. How do I control my anger? Should I consult a psychiatrist? Or do meditation?

A.

Try a meditation technique called gibberish. Or -- find someplace away from others, and beat a pillow on the ground. Really pound it. Don't stop when you feel tired. Keep going and going. Throw all of the anger into the ground, through the pillow. Then, when you are totally exhausted, stop. Lie down on your back. Put a cool, moist towel on your eyes. Breathe into your belly. Put your hands on your heart. Feel the ground supporting you. Let the tension drop out of your body, and feel Love filling you up.

Q.

Why can't I meditate? My cousin sent me meditation videos that she uses, and so I watched them. I do not feel any better: in fact I feel more stressed out now. I tried automatic writing twice, and literally nothing came out. I am pissed off because of my shitty results. What the hell is wrong with me? I could barely shut my eyes, and once I did and started to relax it wasn't great at all.

A.

Whoa. You may be starting with activities (videos, writing) that are ill-suited for you. While I do not know you, it seems from your question you have a lot of pent-up energy. Perhaps a more active technique, like gibberish, will be good to get started.[15]

Q.

I hate this person at my church. This person who talks a lot says that he doesn't let his five year old daughter watch Sponge Bob because it's too violent and "bad." That dirty child "obeser" (obese + abusive because he is fat) just sickens me. I hate him so bad. It's rated Y7-FV. WTF? What a strict parent. He just doesn't know how to be a Christian. What a disgrace to mankind. Who agrees that he is too strict and needs to burn in hell?

A.

I would suggest, instead of judging others as unworthy of being Christian, you have a look at your own words and feelings.

Q.

Am I going crazy? I can be the most random person you ever knew. Sometimes I get REALLY strong impulses to like punch my friend for no reason. Or yell in some random person's face cuz I think it would be funny. I can control most of my impulses. But like to my friend I might say, "I almost kicked you," and he would say "Why?" and I would just say, "impulse."

A.

It sounds like you have a lot of pent up anger, and need a way to express it safely. Why not try gibberish meditation?[16] And please, do not hurt anyone, including yourself. Is there someone around you can talk to, who you trust?

Q.

Is there a cure for worrying and stress? What this question means is that if all other things fail like meditation, relaxation, etc, what can people do to get rid of it? How can people deal with stress in ways that doesn't have to do with medicine, money, doctors, technology or exercise?

A.

When you rule out medicine, doctors, technology, exercise, meditation, and relaxation, you have pretty much ruled out all of the options. It sounds like, unconsciously, you want to remain in stress. Hmmm.....

Q.

I'm always feeling mean, grumpy and complaining. I don't like to be this way all the time. It seems like it's just hard for me to feel optimistic, happy and just decent to be around. How can I change this behavior?

A.

I am a meditator, and it is my experience that I cannot change how I feel. The best I can do is watch, and be present, and accept whatsoever is from my heart. Next, I can find ways to express the feelings in a non-harmful way. Try a meditation technique called gibberish.[17]

5 - Seeing Images

*"When the approaching presence calls out, [Rumi] says,
the first word spoken will coincide exactly with the last
word of his last poem. For Rumi, poetry is what he does
in the meantime, a song-and-dance until the greater reality he loves arrives: a melting tear-gift eye-piece to look
through, while it and the scene and the eye dissolve."[18]*

--Coleman Barks

Q.
What does this particular meditation session mean? I was meditating for about half an hour yesterday, trying to find my power object and my spirit guide. This is what happened: I was sitting in a
forest when I heard a noise so I stood up. As I did I saw a brightly
colored red and gold squirrel on a tree. I walked up to it and it did
not move. I stroked it gently. The squirrel went back onto the tree
and said, "My name is Hephaestus." After many other things happened, I came back to reality.

A.
There are at least two schools of thought about this type of experience.

Some schools, such as several Native American traditions, will as-
sign various meanings to different images: wolf, eagle, etc.

Other schools, such as Zen Buddhism, will suggest that all images,
thoughts, ideas, and feelings are simply "mind stuff." They are
things that float through the mind as you sit and bring awareness to
your inner world.

Since in these schools meditation is all about awareness, about the
witness, about the process of watching itself and being present to
what is, whatever it is, no meaning is attached to the images. One

simply watches: "Aha, a wolf has appeared. Now it is gone. Now my mind is trying to figure out what this means. Is it good? Is it bad?" And so forth.

In Zen, one is simply concerned with noticing whatsoever is happening inside, because it is the *awareness* that is significant. The awareness brings light and godliness into one's life.

Q.
I listened to a guided meditation on YouTube. I think I met my spirit guide but I can't remember her name. I asked was I going to catch the biggest fish out of my group when I go fishing. She said no. Was I imagining stuff or was it real?

A.
This whole spirit guide thing is tricky. There are so many thoughts and images passing through the mind, it is easy to mistake a mind-thing for something beyond. The best thing is to continue to meditate. Watch your thoughts, feelings, and sensations. Over time, you will develop the able to discern what is what in the inner world.

Q.
If you do deep state meditations could spirit guides appear to you without you wanting them to? I was born and raised in a Christian family so I believe that guides are really demons in disguise. I do transcendental meditations from time to time. I have anxiety so this helps me to become much more calm and relaxed. I was curious about trying some deep state relaxation meditations but want to be careful and not mess with anything spiritual.

A.
The deeper you go into meditation, the more and more will be revealed to you about the inner world. As an example, I always thought that I liked myself. After meditating for a while, I realized that what I liked was my accomplishments, but that at a deeper

level, I really *hated* myself. This was quite a shock. I had to drop a lot of beliefs I had about myself and the world.

Meditation has a way of shaking up one's belief systems (in a good way) and opening one's eyes (also in a good way.) And usually, as you move on, you will attract people into your life who can help you deal with any difficulties that may arise. Remember: "The truth shall set you free." Good luck!

Q.

This morning was different from any other meditation session I've had to date. I got to the point where it was almost like a blackout, or a trip in other words. But this was more than a trip it seemed because it felt so real. But in that and after that experience it felt like I was now aware about the workings of everything pretty much. It was a chilling experience. I am not sure what to think of it. My brain is telling me that it was just a trip caused by a natural release of DMT and is nothing more than the result of the chemical effecting my brain. But I feel like it's something more. Can anyone comment?

A.

After a person has been meditating for a while, "gaps" between thoughts begin to appear. This is a good thing. At first, the gaps tend to be very short -- maybe less than a second in duration. But over time, the gaps get longer. As it is a new feeling to be aware without thought, it can feel surprising. And a range of new experiences is possible.

Perhaps this would be a good time in your development to seek a group of meditators to work with, or at least an "older sibling" who has been down the path. If this is not available in your area, a good yoga class or tai chi class could support you as you grow.

Q.

Is it normal to see images during meditation? They're not positive or negative...just images. I don't know what to do.

A.

Yes. The mind is constantly generating all kinds of thoughts and images. You simply be aware; watch all the thoughts and images pass, the way clouds float through an empty sky. Do not try to analyze them. Just watch. And if you notice your mind analyzing, then watch your mind analyzing. It is the witnessing that is significant.

Q.

A person is awake, but day dreaming. Creates a scene in his mind that he can control. Totally counteracts everything around him. This person plays the acting out. Pretty much an illusion. Is this a condition, disease, or meditation?

A.

Your question contains its own answer: you are day-dreaming.

Most of the time, people day-dream when there are things in their lives that are uncomfortable or difficult to face. Perhaps spend a bit of time looking at the relationships and situations in your life, and see if there is anything that fits this description.

Daydreaming is not a condition, disease, or meditation. It is simply a way to escape. So come back! Have a look around, and see if you can address what ails you.

Questioner's Comment: Not what I was looking for. But I wasn't as informative as I should of been.

Q.

I started off with my usual meditation. I opened my third eye, and started to feed my crown chakra. My visuals were as always exciting, seeing different places without my mind wandering. But today I saw a dark, cloudy, shrouded figure in the shape of a man. I saw no arms or legs. It was as if the "man" was wearing the dark clouds. He pointed at me and I heard, "Return" thrice, "The One" thrice, and "Amen Rah" thrice. Can someone tell me if they've had a similar experience of the sort, and/or what does this mean, who is the figure?

A.

With all due respect, I find it hard to believe that you meditate "without your mind wandering." And given that you have written this, I would remind you that the mind is extremely clever and cunning. Remember: the moment an image *says* something, it is just the mind creating a thought. Nothing supernatural here, my friend.

So, please, return to the basics. Watch your mind, watch your emotions, watch the physical sensations, notice if a desire for supernatural experiences arises, strengthen your discernment, and then have a good cup of tea. Soon you will find the extraordinary in the most ordinary of things.

6 - Philosophy vs. Meditation

"Truth is the daughter of inspiration; intellectual analysis and partialized debate keep the people away from the truth. It is like a finger pointing a way to the moon. Do not concentrate on the finger or you will miss all that heavenly glory."[19]

--Bruce Lee

Q.
The science vs. religion debate is something I have struggled with since my days in high school. ... One argument for religion followed swiftly by a counterargument for science, and so on. For instance:

Science: The earth is a planet. It is one planet of billions in the Milky Way galaxy. So then why would God create an entire universe only to focus his attention on humans and the planet Earth? Our actions have an impact on our lives and the lives of those around us, but in the grand scheme of things they are minute, inconsequential and meaningless. Hence morality and religion are products of small minded thinking.

Religion: Humans have to act by certain morals because they are not like animals. They have feelings, thoughts, are capable of reason, self-restraint, and most of all, have free will.

And so on, in a never ending loop. Will somebody please help me find some answers???

A.
I ask you: would you try to use your arms to lift 2,000 pounds? No -- it is asking your arms to do something which they are not designed to do.

You have inside of you a deep longing to touch the Truth. To know it, to feel it, to be nourished by it.

But you are asking your mind, through philosophy, to get you there. And it *never* will. You can ask a million questions, read a zillion books, and you will never find the Truth.

You are asking your arms to lift 2,000 pounds. You are using the incorrect tool for the job.

It is like this: if you are very thirsty, and a glass of water is placed before you, do you think your thirst will be quenched by talking about the water? By thinking about it? No -- you have to drink the water.

Meditation is gathering water from the well. Meditation is drinking the water. Cool, fresh nourishment springing from existence. What bliss. What benediction. All the questions simply disappear, and you melt into the Truth.

Then science can be science. And the scriptures of religion will dissolve into your direct knowing of what is.

Q.
What religion relies the most on internal spiritual thought and meditation?

A.
Do not confuse "internal spiritual thought" with meditation. Meditation has nothing to do with thinking. Meditation brings awareness to thinking, but awareness is beyond the mind.

Thought is not spiritual. At the beginning, thought can be useful. For example, you may want to spend time thinking about your personality, observing how you behave in certain circumstances, etc.

But over time, if you are meditating, your awareness should grow stronger than your thinking.

True religion requires that you go beyond thinking. Into awareness. Consciousness. Blissfulness.

Q.
God is love and if you don't believe in God then you don't love?

A.
I prefer to think of it this way: if you do not love, you cannot know godliness. Belief will not help. Belief is of the mind, and love is of the heart. And you can fill yourself with love by practicing meditation.

Q.
Do Christians believe meditation is against God? Is there any concept of self realization (awakening of spiritual energy) through meditation in Christianity?

A.
Many Christians understand that prayer and meditation are closely related. See the book, The Cloud of Unknowing, written by an unknown Christian mystic. "... the [Christian] work embraces the reader with a maternal call to grow closer to God through meditation and prayer."[20]

Q.
Does anyone believe the world will end in 2012?

A.
2012 is simply another year in which to practice mindfulness.

Q.
I have been struggling with the idea of a God and Jesus and all that jazz. Do you guys think it is real? I don't really know and I am

having a hard time believing it. I am doing much better now than when I was devotedly chasing after a relationship with God. I had too much guilt and felt like I had to be living up to these unrealistic expectations. I have meditated several times but just ended up falling asleep each time haha. What do you all think is a good way of spiritual fulfillment?

A.
I wholeheartedly agree that fixing on a set of beliefs is not the way to go.

Meditation provides a way to look in: to see for yourself what exists in the inner world. Try a technique called gibberish, to deal with the sleeping (best done in the morning).[21]

Q.
Should we choose our beliefs carefully? Can we make our lives a lot more meaningful and joyful just by a diligent selection of belief?

A.
Beliefs will not help. You need to *know.* And the way to knowing is meditation.

Q.
Who is worse, an atheist, or a person who doesn't follow the same religion as you do?

A.
Why does someone have to be "worse?" Why can't we each be unique?

Q.
Can humans completely make up religions and beliefs?

A.

Humans have created all religions and beliefs. There is, however, something which lies beyond humans, and inspires humans, and flows through humans, and informs the greatest teachings: consciousness.

Q.

What would you say Osho's philosophy can be listed under?

A.

Osho did not offer a philosophy. He said this over and over again. Osho offered meditation techniques, so that his disciples could become more aware of what is.

Q.

Why do some people say conscience is 'the voice of God?' I personally think it's just our inner feeling to what is right and wrong. Something that we learn from experience.

A.

I too have found that conscience, as opposed to consciousness, is something we learn from experience. It is conditioning, imposed on us by parents, teachers, and society. It has nothing to do with divinity or godliness. If you wish to know something of the divine, meditate. Become more aware of this very moment. Find a technique that feels right, and jump in!

Q.

Individuality: was it ever really inspired? Artists are inspired by ideas and emotions that are very human. Most art (even abstract) is all just an idea turned outward to reflect your ability to express and convey that idea to others. Regardless of the details, you are simply drawing attention to things that several other human beings before you have put value into.

People like the same old ideas again and again, just changed around a little. Look at every single movie out there, it's the same old story just under a new title. End of rant, feel free to add on...

A.
You are mostly correct, in my opinion. Ideas are mostly borrowed and re-arranged -- products of the mind which is really the Mind of Us All.

To get to freshness, you must transcend mind. Go beyond mind, to awareness. Awareness is divinity. Awareness is godliness. Awareness (colored by mind) is the Muse artists wait for. Awareness is the source of originality, of true individuality.

So stop philosophizing (because you of course are guilty of the very thing you are criticizing). And seek awareness. How? Begin to meditate.

7 - So-Called Spiritual Experiences

"Spiritual truth is not something elaborate and esoteric, it is in fact profound common sense. When you realize the nature of mind, layers of confusion peel away. You don't actually 'become' a buddha. You simply cease, slowly, to be deluded. And being a buddha is not being some omnipotent spiritual superman, but becoming at last a true human being."[22]

--Sogyal Rinpoche

"If you continue practicing simply every day, you will obtain some wonderful power. Before you attain it, it is something wonderful, but after you attain it, it is nothing special."[23]

--Shunryu Suzuki

Q.
How can I get more knowledge on intuition? Can you help me find more articles or books about intuition and guiding dreams?

A.
Reading about intuition and/or guided dreams will not be helpful to you. Most people who think that intuition is happening are being tricked by their minds. And even if someone is writing about their experiences of intuition, it is *their* experience, not yours. Reading about it will actually hurt your chances of becoming more sensitive. Because your mind will now have all kinds of ideas about what may or may not happen, and your mind will create thoughts about these ideas, which will try to fool you into thinking you are being intuitive. Get it?

If you are interested in your inner world, why not try meditation? Over time, your awareness will grow stronger, you will become more sensitive, and you will delight in the mysteries of your inner being!

Q.

I have only chakra meditated three times so I'm new to it and ever since I started I've been feeling more paranoid and feel like someone is watching me. I have had dreams about the future and when I sleep its like I'm half-way asleep and like I'm in two worlds at once and its weird and I hear my name being called and then people whispering. I was wondering if it could be that I am opening my third eye chakra and I have never had this strong of a feelings. Could you please tell what to expect. Please and thank you.

A.

My sense is you might do well to connect with a group of experienced meditators. You don't have to go through this alone.

While it is true that many experiences will happen as your meditation deepens, it is also true that the mind is very clever and cunning. It will try to trick you into thinking things are "happening" when in fact you are just daydreaming and fantasizing. That's why its good to be with folks who have been through the process. They can help you discriminate between what is "real" and what is "mind-stuff."

Q.

In yoga, meditation and relaxation etc, they talk about your body's energy. What is this energy? Is it the same as energy I get from eating spinach or having a glucose drink?

A.

The best thing to do is to simply practice the techniques you are learning. As you do, you may notice all kinds of thoughts, feelings, and physical sensations. Go with your experience, not what "they" say.

Q.
Is there a good website, or book, or whateva that has some detailed instructions on the proper ways to stimulate the chakras when you first start out? Is meditation always required?

A.
Working with chakras is an advanced technique. Strong roots in meditation is a must. One meditation technique is called gibberish.[24]

Q.
How should I begin my satanic power meditation? I'm a new satanist and I want to begin my journey but I'm not sure how to begin? I've bin [sic] told to start power meditation daily but how should I go about doing this?

A.
There is no such thing as "satanic power meditation" or "power meditation." Please drop the word meditation from your pursuits.

What is it that you want so badly, that you would work with a so-called "Satan" to get it?

When I think of Satan, I think of all of the ways in which negativity expresses through a human being. When I feel greed happening, one might say this is Satan expressing through me. When I feel harsh ambition or crass lust arise in myself, it is the darkness of the Universe arising within me.

The question is, what do I do with these very real forces? Do I express them in the world, mistreating my friends, my loved ones, and myself? Or do I find a more constructive way to express and release this energy?

Perhaps I can beat a pillow in anger, or find a secluded place and yell and scream nonsense words at the top of my lungs. These are ways to release the darkness without hurting anyone.

Anything to release the negativity, so that love and delight can arise in my being.

Q.
I feel like I am walking a thin line but I don't want to fall. When does meditation turn into sorcery? I am a Christian. I try to meditate, and sometimes visualize but I don't want it to be any type of sorcery.

A.
Meditation is about witnessing. Watching the mind. There should be no "doing" or "visualization." If you simply watch the mind, body, and emotions, and accept whatsoever is happening from your heart, you will be fine.

Q.
Did I just become an Illuminati pyramid? In my last meditation, my forehead got ignited, but the center of my hands were also ignited. They were the vertices of a triangle. This always happens when I meditate deeply. Could this be the hidden meaning behind the nails in the hands of Jesus? The 'ignited' I'm talking about is electromagnetic energy.

A.
Simply be present to sensation. Do not attach symbol or significance. This too shall pass.

Q.
How can you train your mind for magic and meditation to work for wiccans and witchcraft? I feel witchcraft and magic is for some selfish gain. I have no idea why someone would want to cast a

spell. The only reason is to get something or make something happen in their lives...

So, to 'focus' your mind consciousness and attention on your 'spell' or 'wish' is to make the energy from your mind. I'm confused about the energy? How do u know it is 'energy'? I said this to a classmate in college who is a REAL witch practicing wiccan. I'm worried about what she is up to...

A.
I largely agree with your first paragraph. The only reason to "cast a spell" is because you desire something.

So why do you persist in asking questions about it? It sounds like, underneath, there is some part of you that is interested.... hmmm...? Perhaps you need to look in, and see if the very thing you distrust in your friend is lurking, unseen, inside of you.

Q.
I have a real powerful meditation music that DOES WORK, but I am afraid to get deep into it. I got this idea that a demon might scratch me or I will be somewhere and not find my body again. Can anyone ease these anxieties?

A.
There are all kinds of products out there these days. Some are capable of inducing various trance states or alternate states of consciousness. If you are using music or other products, I would suggest using them in person with an expert who knows the product well. Also, you need to trust the person completely. If these conditions do not exist, I would suggest a more natural approach. Why not try vipassana or gibberish meditation?[25]

Q.
I started meditating for the first time last night and this is what happened....

I couldn't do it at first. After maybe 15 minutes I started to slip into focus and it sounds like you can focus on a lotta different things as long as your mind is totally quiet, so I imagined a ball of energy in my solar plexus that traveled up to my nasal passage when inhaling and going back down into the core in exhaling. Then I started pulsating, it was a very surreal feeling, like I just knew energy was flowing thru me. Especially down my back and head, but even my finger tips. The feeling tapered off after a few seconds. So then I was like, this **** is wild, lets see if I can make it happen again, and I refocused myself, and it immediately began again when I was concentrated.

A.

With all due respect, I find it very hard to believe that all the things you describe happened in your first meditation session. What have you been reading? Borrowed knowledge will *not* help on the path of meditation.

Slow down. Stop imagining you are "making balls of energy" and moving them around, and choose a simple technique to practice on a daily basis.

Q.

How can you tell if you have received cosmic energy from meditation?

A.

It is not essential to be able to label the various things you experience in meditation. What is essential is that you simply watch, you become more aware. Slowly, slowly, you will develop the ability to discriminate amongst the various internal events that happen. And if you notice the mind trying to label or figure things out, watch that: "Interesting, the mind is trying to label. Hmm..."

Q.
I went to my therapist a few months ago, was going though a mid-life crisis at the age of 19, but that's not important. During one of my sessions we did a relaxation and meditation technique.

I laid down as she guided me down stairs into my subconscious. At the end of the meditation I was very deep into it. She told me to picture me laying down, a light above me shining down on me like a spot light. It lifted me up and up and into itself. I physically felt very warm. Something weird happened. Everything was bright. Like I had my eyes closed but someone was shining a bright light on my face.

My therapist hesitated for a moment, then brought me back. I asked what happened. She said and I quote, "I thought I saw a ray." She never brought it up again. What happened?

A.
When I was your age, I went to a healer (a bit more experienced than your therapist) and had a similar experience. It didn't happen again for years, and was never discussed.

What I can say is this. When the time is right (and perhaps the time is now) you will discover meditation. And as you begin to look into your inner world, and develop the tools and strength you need to do so, you will experience all kinds of wonderful mysteries.

For now, let it be.

8 - Desiring Certain Outcomes or States of Being

"You have always been there; it was only desire that was distracting you. Sometimes the desire was for money, sometimes for God, sometimes for power, prestige, sometimes for heaven, paradise, but any desire is enough to distract you from your nature. When there is no desire, where can you go? All desires lead you away from yourself. When there is no desire you are simply centered in your being. That very centeredness is bliss, is ecstasy, is samadhi, is nirvana."[26]

--Osho

Q.
How we can do meditation deeply? How many years does it take a person to reach alpha state during meditation?

A.
It is natural, because you are human, that your mind will try to succeed in meditation. Or it may desire to reach a certain depth, or state of consciousness.

However, please *be present* to these desires, rather than trying to act on them. There is no "correct" state of mind.

Your question indicates a certain impatience, like, "when am I going to get there already?" Impatience, ambition, greed for spiritual experiences: these are all very common parts of the mind, and are things to notice, and accept from your heart. Through this acceptance, slowly slowly, the ego-mind will begin to melt.

Q.

Hey I'm so curious???? Can mantra meditation attract love into your life?

A.

I'm not a big fan of manifesting anything; but in particular, trying to "spell" another person into your love life simply doesn't seem kosher to me.

Open your heart; fill yourself with love (by meditating); and let things happen...and enjoy what is in your life right now!

Q.

I want to learn how to meditate, you know, like activate my chakras. Give me real advice -- no shitty stuff.

A.

The main thing to be understood is to drop the idea of trying to meditate for anything. If you begin by acting on the desire for quieter thoughts or deep calm or "active chakras" or more relaxation or any other things you are setting yourself up for failure.

Simply notice what is, and accept it from your heart, with no expectations for any particular state of being. And if expectations arise, accept them too!

> *[This point is so important, I provide other questions which have the same answer: simply be present to desires as they arise -- do not act on them. As you read the questions, see if you can identify the desires embedded within the questions.]*

Q.

How does a person use meditation to reach "Kundalini?"

Q.

I want to open my third eye -- how do I do it?

Q.

Is it possible to transcend time and see the future when you are in deep meditation?

Q.

How can I get better at self-hypnosis and meditation? How can I go into a deeper relaxation?

Q.

What is cosmic energy? Is it really available in meditation?

Q.

Can I use meditation to unlock tele-kinesis?

Q.

I'm looking for two types of meditation. One where I can possibly astral project, or just control a dream, and another that will raise my consciousness.

Q.

I have been practicing mediation and have been learning to relax and calm myself. I'm still finding it hard to plow into a deep meditative state. Any tips or good cds or anything to help achieve this would be great.

A.

One of the most important things as you move along the path of meditation is patience. You are inviting the light of awareness (which is to say godliness, or divinity) to surround you and melt away all that is dark and useless.

The darkness comes in many forms: lust, greed, ambition, fear, and so forth. There are many layers of the unconscious that will need to be seen and accepted from the heart.

The process is most effective if there is no *doing* involved. In fact, *you* cannot do anything. It is the *you* that is the problem. When you watch (which is part of every meditation technique) you are bringing awareness to the thoughts and feelings inside... the watching, the witnessing is not you -- it comes from beyond you.

So -- when you notice thoughts like, "I find it hard to plow into..." (which is a very active, assertive idea), or "how do I achieve this state?" (which indicates a desire for a certain kind of experience), be alert. This is the mind coming in, trying to take over a process which it knows nothing about.

When these thoughts arise, bring consciousness to them. The thoughts are sign posts which will lead the awareness to the places inside of you which need light.

Q.
If I sit in meditation for a long enough time, will I induce an "altered state of consciousness." If this is not how to induce an altered state, then how?

A.
If you practice meditation, you will experience something better than an altered state of consciousness. You will experience true bliss. You will experience the Real. You have the chance of tasting godliness. Why would you want an "altered state of consciousness" when you have the chance to taste the divine itself?

But -- there is a trap here. If you desire these things when meditating, you will push them away. You must begin at the beginning, with witnessing. Be present to the desires which arise, rather then acting on them.

Q.

I suck at meditating. It took me an hour before I decided to quit trying desperately to meditate successfully. Although, there was a time within that hour that I felt three things: 1) My head felt fuzzy; 2) I could feel my body heat rise; 3) Even though I was sitting straight up, I felt as though I was laying down. Would this be considered successful meditation?

A.

Whoa...slow down.

It is natural, because you are human, that your mind will try to succeed in meditation. However, please *be present* to these desires, rather than trying to act on them. There is no "correct" state of mind.

Questioner's Comment: okay ty, I won't try so hard to alter my state of consciousness.

Q.

I have always been sensitive to the presence of ghosts and spirits and recently have been trying to develop this and contact my spirit guide using meditation. I simply CANNOT meditate at all, trying to look up at my "3rd eye" just hurts my eyes and other times I just see black and get bored. The only thing I kinda saw was a pair of eyes with big eyelashes, they kinda flashed like a shadow out of the dark behind my eyes then went away in a flash.....is this anything?

A.

I have no doubt that you are very sensitive. And it is certainly the case that one's awareness can perceive very subtle mental, emotional, and physical sensations.

The reason you are finding it difficult to meditate is that you are trying to meditate *for* something.

Over time, you will develop a finer and finer "discernment" -- the ability to discriminate between a thought, a feeling, and a sensation. It has been my experience (after 15 years of watching) that 98% of what I "see" is simply mind doing its thing...

Questioner's Comment: Thanks, I guess I need to do some research on meditation before I jump into it :P

Q.
I'm very interested in meditation but there are so many different ways out there. Some say that you must be at peace and quiet, not make any noise or movement or even pay attention to your breathing and to be comfortable, meanwhile others say you should chant something or "aum," and be completely conscious of your breathing etc...

It's frustrating and I don't know where to begin. I really want to work on opening my third eye, and I want to know which type of meditation is best for this.

A.
The first thing: "really wanting to work on your third eye" is a wrong-headed way to approach meditation. You may desire all kinds of things when you begin, but please be present to these desires rather than acting on them.

The unconscious (that is, the negative energy inside of all of us) takes all kinds of forms: lust, greed, anger, ambition, and so forth. Greed, for example, may be directed at wealth, or power, or experiences of various kinds. The meditator is interested in noticing his greed, and bringing heartful awareness to it. Over time, by itself (not because *you* do it) the greed will begin to dissolve in the presence of awareness, and the energy will be transformed into compassion and generosity.

Questioner's Comment: "I see"... said the blind man.

9 - Physical Sensations

"When you meditate, try to allow whatever arises to move through you as it will. Let your attention be very kind. Layers of tension will gradually release, and energy will begin to move. Places in your body where you have held the patterns of old illness and trauma will open. Then a deeper physical purification and opening of the energy channels will occur as the knots release and dissolve. Sometimes with this opening we will experience a powerful movement of the breath, sometimes a spontaneous vibration and other physical sensations."[27]

--Jack Kornfield

Q.

I have recently begun meditating and sometimes I find it difficult as I get an intense 'tingling' sensation between my eyes and a similar sensation around my throat. This makes it difficult to concentrate on my breathing and, ultimately, relax.

A.

My guess is you are doing a quiet meditation, such as vipassana (watching the breath). With what is happening, you might want to try a more active meditation, to get your energy moving. One such meditation technique is called gibberish.[28]

Q.

I have just taken 30 mg of oxycontin and 10 mg of valium at the same time. Will I be alright? Also I am wondering what the safe amount of magic mushrooms (Psilocybin) is to take for a first time because I want to use it for meditation.

A.

You are playing with fire, my friend. Do not proceed down the path you are walking. Do not mix these drugs. And do not add meditation into the mix.

Q.

Last night I meditated just prior to going to bed; the meditation felt (it's tough to describe) deeper, less chatter going on in my head, almost touching blissful and everything was great. However, once in bed I couldn't sleep. It wouldn't bother me if it did, but I'm just wondering if meditation can affect your sleep?

A.

Yes, meditation can effect sleep patterns. My suggestion is to meditate upon waking up, or around sunset (6 or 7 pm) but not later than that. And if you are meditating in the evening, only do quiet meditations (like vipassana), not active, or cathartic techniques.[29]

Q.

Why do I need to rest my back while doing a one hour meditation? I prefer to have a wall against my back to support it.

A.

I always need a back support, and many others do too. Just keep your back straight, using pillows or other comfy devices.

Q.

Why do I cry during meditation? I feel these intense vibrations and cooling feeling over my body but for some reason tears fall from my eyes. I don't sob it's just they flow. Why is it that this happens?

A.

Do not be concerned. Simply allow the body to do what it does.

Q.

One of my relatives was a Buddhist monk who moved here from Mongolia a couple months ago. He invited me to fast with him to "help reach enlightenment" and "purify our bodies." I've been drinking a lot of (organic) citronella and green tea and water, and I've also been doing light yoga exercises as well as meditation. I start medical school in September. Less than a year ago I gave birth to a son. I'm doing this mostly for the "educational" experience: I'm planning to study abroad in China (and stay at a Buddhist monastery for two weeks) next summer. Do you think there's any real truth to "detoxing" or anything like that, including a spiritual part of it?

A.

There are all kinds of detox-ing methods out there, and yes, many of them work. However, I'm a bit concerned about your timing. It sounds like you have not been meditating for long. With a fast like this, much can shift in your "normal waking consciousness," and it is very important to have a strong grounding in meditation, to deal with the shifts. Also, since you are soon to start medical school (a very stressful activity) it might not be the right timing to do such a strong detox. And, on top of it all, you have a young child! Go slow to go fast. (Pun intended ;-))

Q.

Is a slight pain-like feeling in the forehead after meditation normal? I try to keep the focus between my eyes. I have a wonderful feeling after that. But there is a slight pain-like feeling probably because I bring my eyes close together. Is it normal?

A.

In my opinion, you need to be very careful with any meditation technique that involves exercises with the eyes. This is a *very* delicate area of the body, and requires much caution.

If you feel *any* discomfort at all, *stop doing the technique.*
Wait for a few days. Then go back to doing a softer technique, like
vipassana, for a few weeks.[30]

Q.
Meditation is amazing! I've been meditating for a month or so but
last night I really got in the "zone" and I had a erection and it felt
like I was having a mini orgasm or on a drug or something it was
crazy then I just lied down and went to sleep.

A.
It is good that you had an enjoyable experience. But remember,
this too shall pass. The important thing now is not to desire a re-
play of the event. All kinds of things will happen as you go deeper
into meditation. Simply stay present to whatever is happening
in this moment, and do not cherish the things that have happened
in the past.

Q.
Cannot meditate / eyes tremble! HELP!? I tried meditating; I've
got a Master Choa Kok Sui instructional CD. Whenever I close
my eyes, they sort of tremble, and I just cannot seem to focus on
anything but that at the moment. I asked my mom what's going on,
since she's done this meditation for quite a while. Response? I
heard words such as idiot, imbecile, liar, self-destructive, etc.
hurled at me. So can anyone please help me. I'm getting quite depressed and sick of doing everything I do 'the wrong way.'

A.
If ever you begin to feel any kind of discomfort from meditating,
the safest thing to do is simply stop for a while. Do not listen to
your mother. Trust your body and instincts.

Q.
Meditation energy stuck? When I meditate I feel energy stuck on
my face especially on my jaw. I don't know how to release it us-

ing Reiki healing or other methods. Could anyone tell me how to use Reiki to release the energy on my jaw?

A.

It is beautiful that you are aware of this phenomena. My suggestion is to continue to do the meditation technique you are using, and simply watch what is happening around your jaw. Do not try to change or fix it. Simply accept it from your heart. Remember to breathe. Bring a gentle awareness to your jaw. It may stay the same, and it may change. But allow this to happen on its own. *You* simply be present.

Q.

Where on the body r the vibrations felt in meditation? I felt weird feelings in my stomach and torso area. Was that the vibrations? Also, it feels like warm waves are emitting throughout my brain. My head moves all of a sudden from one side or to the other. My eyebrows raise by themselves. My arms start to get numb. Also, there is heat release throughout my body.

A.

It depends on where you are in the process. Early on, the mind can trick you. You have probably heard all kinds of stories about vibrations and kundalini and this and that. So the mind takes a common stomach ache and turns it into a spiritual experience.

Watch! Be aware of what the mind is doing. Discriminate...

And then, if these things are still happening, know that they can happen anywhere in the body. My suggestion to you is that you find someone local to you who is an experienced meditator. When things like this begin happening on the path, it is good to have someone around who has "been there."

If the sensations get too intense, stop meditating for a few days. And if in the moment things don't cool down, take a cold shower. Literally. Believe me, it helps.

Questioner's Comment: Wow... I never thought about that. Nice work. Imma google some one right now thanks a lot.

[A few people wrote about their insomnia. The best thing I have found is a supplement called melatonin. It is available in most health food stores.]

10 - More Advanced Questions

"The Path that leadeth on is lighted by one fire -- the light of daring burning in the heart. The more one dares, the more she shall obtain."[31]

--Helena Petrova Blavatsky

"If you do not understand, you should not speak, for that is only blood dripping.

It is better for you to keep your mouth shut as spring passes."[32]

--Zen Master Seung Sahn Soen-sa

Q.
What are your personal experiences of meditating? What were you like before and after? Did it change your way of thinking? Please don't write what you've read about; I only want personal experiences. Thank you.

A.
It is a beautiful and perceptive question.

Before I started, I was very mind-y, and constantly doing. I was committed to a career, to getting successful. I was empty inside and often unhappy.

Now, 15 years later, I have many moments of blissfulness throughout the day. My mind is still very active, but I am often aware of it. And at times I have space from it. It does its thing, but it does not always run me. And simply seeing it for what it is brings more truth into my world.

My desires and ambitions have slowly slowly faded away (just as the Buddha said they would). I do not need as many material things to live, because I have seen that they do not provide lasting contentment.

Sitting in a restaurant,
a child walks by,
and smiles.

Our eyes meet, our faces light up.
So much love.
What more is needed?

These are a few of my experiences. But they will not be yours. Are you ready to begin meditating yourself? Because anything you read is simply borrowed knowledge. You must begin to meditate on your own to find your own way.

Q.
I basically pay attention to what my mind is doing like in mindful meditation BUT I use "self talk" to describe it! So if I'm aware of anxiety or a negative thought I say, "ah, there's anxiety or there's a negative thought," and it goes away! I realize I haven't transcended the false self this way but it's so much easier for me to narrate the contents of my mind than be perfectly silent and perfectly aware. So what am I doing!?

A.
You have stumbled on an old Buddhist technique. When you notice anger, simply say to yourself, "anger anger." If you notice sadness, say to yourself (not out loud) "sadness sadness." When thoughts are happening, say "thinking thinking." And so on....
Over time, gaps may arise in your thought process, and you will

have more glimpses of a blissful silence. The technique is not pure awareness, but it is a mind-technique to help you to move towards pure awareness. Take care!

Questioner's Comment: WOW This really works well! Thanks mate!!! :)

Q.
Does meditation work and treat ADHD, without harmful drugs? I have been feeling lonely and crying a lot...

A.
I have been diagnosed by Western doctors with bipolar, and I have been meditating for 15 years. I can say with utmost certainty that meditation helps.

A few things. You probably want to start with active (rather than passive) techniques. There are techniques that allow you to move, to throw off excess energy, before sitting and going in. One such technique is called gibberish.[33]

As you go deeper in your practice of meditation, you will become aware of more and more stuff. And not all of it is roses!

The thing is -- keep practicing. Continue to eat healthy, drink lots of water, and do your technique. If you feel like crying, cry! Crying is a great way to move stuck energy. You might even put on some sad music to aid the process.

If you feel lonely, this is a very good sign. Because in fact you are alone. We all are. When we first see it, it is uncomfortable. But over time your loneliness will morph into aloneness: a profound sense of contentment with who you are, just as you are, all by yourself.

Another thing: remember that the collective is nuts! The people around you are freaking out about terrorism and the economy and global warming. And if your practice is deepening, you will begin to feel this collective angst more and more. Just be present in each moment, keep breathing, and notice what is happening.

Also, it is probably best to work with a teacher or a group of people, rather than on your own. That way, if stuff comes up, you have a place to turn. (Mention to the group leader that you have been diagnosed by Western doctors as having ADHD. You might also want to share this message with him/her.)

Over time, meditating gives you space from the chattering mind. So the active mind may continue with its thoughts, but you will be able to watch them from a distance. They will not disturb you as much. Good luck!

Q.
What r some natural ways to help with bi-polar? Examples: herbs... meditation techniques....etc....

A.
Gibberish.[34]

Q.
Could yoga be used to help kids with ADD?

A.
Yes.

Q.
Do you think meditation can help me become less of a dick? I'm bipolar but I hate the drug effects on me, so I don't use it. I seem to blow on every stupid question my family asks me.

A.
Hi. I am a bipolar meditator on meds.

Yes, meditation can help a lot. But please, in the beginning, stay on your meds. It seems clear from the research that there is a bio-chemical component to bipolar. And the meds help stabilize at that level. Perhaps it is possible for your doc to lower the doses, or give less?

Over time, meditation helps you become less attached to your mind and emotions, so even as you swing from manic to depression, it has less effect on you. You don't act on it as much, and it does not bother you as much.

Q.
Should we change our strategy for treating patients with anxiety disorders? Most of the times a patient having an anxiety disorder is prescribed a SSRI. I think ideally treatment should consist of counseling, CBT, taking patients' relatives in confidence and training the patient about meditation and relaxation. What are the views of experts and patients?

A.
More meditation! The mental health field needs more like you.

Q.
I can become aware of any anxiety or negative emotion when I'm alone and it just evaporates.

But in public the thoughts are so rapid and the feelings so intense I get drawn into them and I can't stay aware for very long. How do I not get taken over by them when they are so intense and so rapid?

A.

It takes practice and patience. But it is beautiful that you are think-ing about it. My master talks about "taking meditation into the marketplace."

For me, what works is to start with little things, like being present when you are brushing your teeth, or washing the dishes. Then you can try it while waiting at the bus stop.

And pat yourself on the back for the small successes. Even being aware for three seconds during the work day is a big thing. Good luck!

Q.

Is meditation futile if you still have an ego for a centre? Or will the awareness of the ego during meditation be enough? Also, is the ego a thought? It feels like it's bigger than a thought.

A.

We all have egos when we start meditating. The ego is a collection of thoughts, feelings, and sensations which, when taken together, we call "I" or "myself." One characteristic of the ego is that it is almost always desiring something. Many meditators start out with their egos desiring enlightenment.

The trick is to be aware of any thoughts, feelings, or sensations that arise during meditation. When you are being aware of these things, you are being aware of the ego.

Q.

What is non dualistic thinking?

A.

"Non dualistic thinking" is a contradiction in terms.

Thinking, by its very nature, is dualistic. What is the meaning of "up" without the concept of "down?" How can we know "black" without "white?" Thinking happens in the mental realm, which is firmly placed in the world of duality.

The only way I know of to go beyond duality is by meditating. One strengthens one's awareness, so one can become a witness to thoughts, feelings, and physical sensations.

I have been meditating for fifteen years, and I see that I cannot find the words to describe the conditions needed for existing beyond duality. I had better get back to meditating!

Q.
Is meditation helped by a particular kind of diet?

A.
Yes. However, one needs to proceed with a bit of caution. Make changes to your diet slowly, altering one thing at a time, giving your body time to adjust. Go with what feels right, not with any ambition or impatience of the mind.

Ultimately, you want to move towards organic veggies, rice, miso soup, almond milk instead of dairy milk, little or no meat, tofu and beans-and-rice for protein (those meatless meats in the natural foods section are a great source of protein too).

A word on the vegetarian piece: for me, there are three reasons. One is the aesthetics: charred flesh is not beautiful to me. Another is this: I ask myself, "can I imagine preparing a food from start to finish?" That is, with a carrot, I can imagine planting, watering, picking, cleaning, and eating. But a cow? Hmmm....

Thirdly, I have found that eating less meat keeps my whole system lighter, which helps with the meditation.

Q.
Meditation to reveal our unconditioned nature? In meditation, if we discard all thoughts images words feelings and keep discarding no matter how long it takes until we perceive of nothing -- is that the point where true Self meets or reveals itself?

A.
Hi -- the difficulty with your question is the phrase, "if we discard." Who is this "we" who is doing the discarding? It is just another part of the mind, which is the source of thoughts.

In meditation, one simply brings awareness to whatsoever is, with no desire for any particular state of mind. No desire for nothingness or bliss or Nirvana or No-Self. One simply watches.

Over time, much will be revealed. But *you* cannot do anything to make it happen.

Q.
How does one attain and maintain a pure state of mind? Most people can't help but get sexually excited or disgusted at the sight of a naked body or the prospect of sex.

The problem that creates problems is the way we respond to certain things externally. In the underworld of our mind there is a lot going on that we are not aware of. It all stems from childhood trauma's and/or beliefs that were rammed into our head. Our desires will often spiral outward and create problems throughout one's life by neurosis. So how does one attain a correct state of mind?

We do intense meditation to the point where we can build a good solid focus then we use our mind to maintain the "awareness" identity while running through scenarios and let our mind respond as such, being aware of any disgusting or tantalizing desires and negative or positive thoughts without a sense of bias to either side.

Awareness alone could extinguish the ego and any unhealthy desires. There is a way to reach a state of purity.

A.

In my opinion, there is some accuracy in your description of ego mind and its functioning. You are seeing some of what is going on inside, and this is a big step.

However, there are a few misunderstandings in your description of meditation and awareness.

Do not attempt to use meditation to create "a good solid focus." Focus is a quality of the mind, and meditation is all about awareness, not mind.

Also -- there is no such thing as an "awareness identity." Awareness is beyond the mind, and therefore beyond identity. Awareness is gentle; it is soft; it is like a mirror; a witness; a gentle, heartful presence.

One part of your ego mind you may like to bring awareness to is the judge part. You use many words like disgusting, and its opposite, purity. Become aware of this harsh judge. Then take a deep breath and relax.

If you notice an ambition to reach a state of purity, be present to it. It is the heartful, non-judging acceptance that, slowly, slowly, over time, will transform you. What will NOT transform you is a desire for more purity.

Q.
Why does meditation help one focus one's mind on a goal/ ambition?

A.

In my opinion, meditation does not focus one's mind on a goal or ambition. Meditation is about seeing that ambition does not help. Meditation is about seeing goals are creations of the mind, and therefore distract you from the existential direction of your life.

Q.

I have been experiencing symptoms of spiritual awakenings - feelings of rushing energy surges while sleeping, hot hands and feet, tunes in my head, vivid and meaningful realistic dreams, new body adjustments, creative drawings, new perspectives, and spiritual symbols and signs.

The problem is that two weeks ago I was a stubborn atheist. So yeah, I'm extremely new to this.

The thing is, is that I am very eager and ambitious to learn more about meditation, prayer, and basically everything about the subject. Is there any website that is good for beginners? Something that explains the higher organization of things? I understand that all souls of all races/worlds may live a few physical lives and each time it is decided between our spirit and God. From the looks of it, our soul is constantly evolving after each life, is that correct?

A.

A lot is happening for you very quickly. It is good, but please... GO SLOW.

Looking at web sites isn't a terrible thing, but the trap there is that your mind will latch onto the information, and convince you it is happening, when existentially it may not be. (Like when a medical student gets every disease she studies!) Do not spend too much time studying them. Stay with your own experience.

The most important thing you can do at this stage is develop a regular meditation regimen. I will suggest a few simple techniques below. Do one of them every day, in the morning or at sunset.

Also, you might consider looking around at local meditation groups. You do not need to go through this transition alone. Sit in on a class. If your heart expands, this is a good sign. If it contracts, not so much.

You mention you are eager and ambitious. The best thing to do is notice when you feel these things, and watch them, rather than act on them. An ambitious meditator is headed for a very dark road. After all, meditation is all about *melting* ambition (and other forms of unconsciousness). Now, you will continue to feel ambitious, because you are human. But you do not have to act on it. You can slow down, and watch.

Don't worry about systems of thought which try to organize things. There are a million of them out there, and they are all mind stuff. True spirituality goes beyond mind. Bring your attention to strengthening your awareness, your presence in the here-and-now, and your heartfulness.

One meditation technique is called vipassana. Another is called gibberish.[35]

Questioner's Comment: Thank you so much for your input. I was going way too fast with all of this stuff. Now I am slowing down and becoming more aware. Thanks and God bless.

Q.
Are there any meditations or anything of the sort that could teach you techniques how to get questions answered via the subconscious? I have already heard of "pendulum dowsing" but are there ANY other techniques? Thanks!

A.

The best way to discover what is in the subconscious is to make it conscious. To become conscious of more and more of your inner world. And the way to do this is via meditation.

One other piece: the subconscious is dark and unlit. Why would you want questions answered from darkness? No -- simply meditate, bring light to your inner world, and wait for the clarity of awareness to resolve your concerns.

Q.

I went through a really tough time. Was doing drugs and experienced depersonalization. I started getting into spirituality. I read the Power of Now and practiced every day for a year on clearing my mind/ego. I completely got rid of my sense of self which can be a good thing but also a very strange/scary experience. This may sound a bit crazy but I want to figure out how to get my mind going again. Time is frozen and everything is very slow. Kinda like a picture frame. Does anyone know the trick to switching back into the ego state. I know there is no one "right" way to live. I just kinda feel stuck in this timeless meditation state. Please don't answer saying that this is a perfectly fine way to live. I don't want to be a monk or Eckhart Tolle! Thank you all.

A.

The mind is very clever and cunning. Be alert!

You say you completely got rid of your sense of self, and you also say this is a very strange/scary experience. Who is feeling the fear? Who is feeling strange? The witness? Cosmic consciousness? I don't think so. If you are still feeling fear, then *you* still are. You still exist. No selflessness here.

Sorry to burst your bubble.

As for a slow mind: why not go to a health food store with a good supplement section. They have supplements which can support healthy mind functioning.

One more thing. Reading Tolle and others is fine, but beware: the mind will remember what they said, and try to trick you into thinking you are experiencing the same things. Keep meditating, keep watching, keep looking in at your own mind, your own emotions, and see if you can notice the part of the mind which thinks, "ah, now I am having a great experience. Now I notice that time seems slow. ..." If you are alert, you may discover a new, subtle piece of the ego-mind which can be called the spiritual ego.

Q.
When meditating, should it be in 1st person or 3rd person point of view? When I meditate, it's always in a 3rd person point of view (POV). I have to struggle with much effort to get into, and remain in, a 1st person POV. Then, it occurred to me that I hadn't really thought about which way it should be, or if it even matters. Is there a preferred POV during meditation?

A.
Your question points to an interesting issue. I would phrase it this way: who is watching? Who is observing the thoughts, feelings, and physical sensations that pass through the body-mind?

Most people have many different "I"s inside of them. There is the helpful "I", the judging "I", the 'figure out what is happening' "I", the feeling-helpless "I", and so forth. Throughout the day, these "I"s go on changing without being noticed.

Meditation connects the meditator to "the witnessing consciousness." Another name is "awareness." The witness is pure consciousness, residing beyond all of the "I's" associated with ego-mind. One of its properties is its ability to be present to, or "see" that which is going on in the inner world.

.

So, in your terms, the trick is to connect with the witness, and watch or be present to whosoever is observing things: the 1st person POV, the 3rd person POV, the part of the mind trying to figure all of this out, and so forth. *ALL* of these are parts of the mind, and may be watched by the witness, the pure awareness, that is beyond the mind.

Q.
How do you get rid of negative energy? I have been talking to psychics and they say that I have negative energy between my heart and stomach.

A.
A good technique to move energy is called gibberish.[36]

Q.
Is meditation somehow "selfish?" Some of the texts I've read about reaching an "enlightened state" describe it as achieving a deep revelation about your being, and the beauty and interconnectedness of the natural world. The authors refer to a similar experience of "dying," before being reborn in an enlightened form.

While the idea of living in bliss sounds exquisite, I get the vague impression that people like the authors walk around in a kind of blissful stoned stupor. I can't help feeling that this state, although deeply fulfilling, is, in another sense, selfish. I get the sense that people in this enlightened state see the world too radically different to be able to properly interact with their families and friends.

For instance, if your son is sick with cancer, would an enlightened person revive the part of his or her ego that puts up a fight against the disease, and helps support his/her family, or would that person simply say "The cancer is beautiful, and death is a necessary part of life," all the while leaving his/her family in the lurch?

Could becoming enlightened mean attaining personal bliss at the detriment of others' happiness? Is it somehow selfish to become enlightened?

A.

How does one know what do to in a given situation? For me, the answer is, one needs to bring a tremendous amount of consciousness to the moment. Then, divinity will flow through you, and you will take the right action.

Now -- how to gather consciousness? Meditate. Become "enlightened."

Think of love as an analogy. It may sound like a cliché, but you cannot love someone if you are not filled with love yourself.

You cannot be of service in any way (large or small) until you have attained to higher consciousness. And the rare few who have attained to enlightenment have become pure light, pure delight. In my opinion, it is very difficult to comprehend how they operate, what they see, and how they move. And -- it is not my job.

It is my job to meditate. To raise my consciousness, so that, more and more, in each moment, I have a chance to respond with clarity and beauty and harmony. So that my choices align with the incredibly complex mix of seen and unseen influences at play. Simply being smart, and using my mind to weigh the pros and cons, will not be enough. One needs pure consciousness to guide one, and once again, this is obtained through meditation.

So, no, it is not selfish. It is the most selfless thing in the world to meditate.

Questioner's Comment: This is the answer I was waiting for! Thank you!

Q.
Zen Master Kyong Ho asked Zen Master Hahn Am,

"Somebody hears, 'Cloud appears over South Mountain, rain over North Mountain' and gets enlightenment. What do they attain?"

Zen Master Hahn Am replied, "In front of the meditation rooms there are many roof tiles."

Commentary
If you see something, you become blind. If you hear something, you become deaf. If you open your mouth, you become mute. Without making anything, you already find a good answer.

A.
To me, this story is about mind. How mind gets in the way of seeing clearly. In the same way clouds make it hard to see the open sky.

The clouds and rain represent the thoughts in your mind. While thoughts are there, you cannot simply be, resting in clear awareness. The roof tiles are another reference to mind.

Note the commentary: seeing, hearing, and speaking all involve mind: therefore, they obscure you from clarity. When the mental ceases, clarity comes.

Q.
Which is more effective in producing inner peace - meditation or positive affirmations?

A.
Working with positive affirmations is like humming a lullaby while standing on a noisy street. You are trying to cover over the chaos with a little melody. It does not work.

Meditation is the process of learning how to be present to what is, without judgment. At first, you will notice all kinds of thoughts, emotions, and physical sensations. Simply allow them. Over time, "gaps" will appear (just as once in a while there is a pause in the traffic on a street) and a profound sense of peace will descend upon you.

Q.
How should one deal with all the mental clutter? I have all these thoughts in my head about everything and I don't understand what is it I should actually do or what I really want to do. I end up playing video games or watching movies to escape those problems. And that's usually a waste of precious time. Meditation hasn't helped.

A.
This is a beautiful, clear question.

We all have mental clutter. It is the nature of mind. I too (and most of us) get fed up with it and distract myself with TV and other stuff.

There is a place of peace at our innermost core. But we have to address the issue of the mind to access it.

It is like a river. Suppose a horse walks through a river, stirring up all kinds of mud. The water will be unclear -- not very enjoyable. But if we sit by the side of the river, and wait, and watch, eventually the mud will settle, and we will have clear, fresh water again.

The trick is to simply watch. If we try to *do* something, we will just end up stirring up more mud!

The reason meditation has not helped you, I am guessing, is because you were trying to stop the mind, or change it, or fix it. The knack is: simply watch.

Keep breathing, and watching, and eventually, gaps will arise in the thought process. These gaps are the clear, fresh water. And once you have tasted it, you will never turn back.

Q.
I'm an advanced Pranic energy healer. How can I be a better energy healer? I mean are there any specific books or meditations I can benefit from?

A.
My experience with healers is as they go deeper, their intuition guides them to the resources (human and printed) which they need to progress.

My suggestion to you is to meditate more. I suspect, since you do energy work, that you already do meditate. So I would suggest, rather than pursuing improvement as a healer, you go deeper into your meditation. Perhaps your next steps will be revealed there.

Q.
How to separate You from mind/body? How do you create the space between the real you and the mind which is accumulated thoughts?

A.
All meditation techniques strengthen awareness. And as awareness grows, you begin to see that you are not the mind, not the body, not the emotions.

But -- it is not "you" who is creating the separation. And please, do not *try* to create the separation. Simply choose a good technique, and watch the body-mind. Allow the process to unfold naturally.

Q.
All about Eckhart Tolle and his amazing book The Power of Now.
What is the relationship between meditation and seeking your
higher self? How about for those Catholics who seek true happi-
ness? Can we relate these "principles of being" to the teachings of
Jesus Christ?

A.
There is a complete and total relationship between meditation and
seeking your higher self.

When you meditate, you watch your thoughts, feelings, and sensations. Slowly, you begin to see that none of these are yourself. As
you come to know this (from experience), the little "I" dissolves,
making room for the Big "I" (the higher self, or better, pure awareness) to dwell inside of your body-mind.

Catholics can absolutely relate the teachings of Tolle to the teachings of Jesus Christ. There are many examples, but I will take one.
Jesus taught us, "to be in the world without being of the world."

What does this mean? For me, this means live totally, fully in the
world. Enjoy the fruits of the world. Celebrate, love, be compassionate and friendly towards others. Partake of the material things
in the world.

But -- always remember that you are not "of" the world. That there
is an aspect of yourself (we can call it the higher self or pure
awareness) which is beyond the 3-D world. Buddha spoke of being
detached, or dis-identified from the world. You do not cling to the
things in the world. You learn that attachment to desire for things
leads to suffering.

Catholics bring this teaching into the world through the practice of
lent. When someone gives up something for lent, one is question-
ing the notion that they have to have this thing to be happy, or to

be close to God (or godliness). One is asked to look directly into one's desires, and to see if they are real. If one meditates on the desire for the thing which one is giving up for lent, one has the opportunity to see, understand, and ultimately dissolve the root-cause of the desire.

There are other examples (which Tolle mentions in his book -- he quotes Jesus throughout). So have fun exploring this beautiful work.

Q.
Is meditation a way to come to terms with your mortality? Is it a way to quiet your mind and sort of prepare for a loss of existence?

A.
An excellent question. There is only one certainty, and that is death. In a way, life can be looked at as simply a preparation for death. Meditation, at its deepest level, is a little death: the death of the ego, of the personality. You come to know, as your awareness strengthens, that you are not the mind, not the emotions, not even the body. In fact, "you" are not!!!

And once you truly see this, you befriend death. You are no longer afraid of it, so you can then (and only then) live your life to the fullest, squeezing every bit of juice from every moment.

Questioner's Comment: You understand where I come from.

Q.
We'd be spiritual if we didn't have to eat to be alive?

A.
This is a beautiful question. Many people can be spiritual, so long as their basic needs are being met. But what happens when survival issues come in? Can we still remember to breathe? To wait for the winds of existence to blow us into action? Or do we become

greedy and ambitious again? When the survival needs start coming up, it is a true test of the depth of one's spirituality.

Q.

If I color outside the lines can I still get into Heaven?

A.

Coloring outside the lines is the *only* way to get into "heaven."
Just do so in a way that is respectful of others. One other point: in
my view, there is actually no heaven. There is, however, blissfulness, which can be attained through meditation.

Q.

I enjoy meditating, but would like to find a way of doing it in the
midst of my daily activities (while doing my chores, errands, etc.).
How can I learn how to do that? Thanks ;)

A.

What a fantastic question! Yes -- bring your meditation into the
marketplace!

The first thing: slow down. It is much easier to stay present to each
gesture throughout the day if you move at a slower pace.

Next -- you can make little games for yourself. For example, if you
wear a pair of shoes which make a "clack" sound as you walk, you
can say to yourself, "every time I hear the clack sound, I will become aware of my feet hitting the ground."

Another good thing to do is come back to your breath -- at the start
of the day, make it your goal for the day, at each moment, before
lifting a pencil, before starting your car, before dialing a phone
number, you will stop and notice your next three breaths.

I find it is helpful to change the game each day, because the mind
gets used to the idea, and then I forget.

Also, posting little notes around the places I look regularly helps me to remember.

Q.
I have been meditating for years, and my intuition tells me that I need to "listen to my heart" - and well, there is a problem - my heart doesn't speak in words for one thing, and for another - it seems to be really blocked off - I suffered a serious heartbreak a few months ago, and it would seem my "heart" has walled itself shut. How can I "gain access" to it again? So that I can be more open in the future? Thanks all. Be well.

A.
It is beautiful you see that "the heart doesn't speak in words." This is not a problem! This is clear insight.

For me, "listening to my heart" means first tuning into my heart, and then allowing an idea for movement to enter my mind (for example, "I think I'll have Chinese food for dinner.") If I feel a gentle expansion from my heart, or a movement of energy outwards, for me, this is my heart saying yes. If I feel a contraction, and no energy moving, this is a no.

As far as the heartbreak, might I suggest a cathartic meditation? There are many, but why not try gibberish.[37]

Q.
Has my promiscuity in childhood made me the way I am? I started making out with boys in pre-school and I remember faintly that I was lying naked on top of a boy when we were around five. I'm an adolescent now and I've been depressed for a few years and have a high sexual drive, but I don't really act on it. If that stuff didn't happen when I was a kid, would I be less torn up on the inside?

A.

It is totally natural for a human being to feel attracted sexually to others. It is the most basic, most powerful energy in a human: the drive to reproduce. However, our society has imposed all kinds of rules, which force us to suppress this energy. It is these rules that create the problem.

You see, if you feel the energy move you towards hugging a boy, and you get yelled at by your parents or teachers, then you have to suppress the energy (or something bad will happen). Now, over and over, you are suppressing your life energy. Over time, this energy gets "balled up" inside, gets stuck, and has nowhere to move. This leads to the feelings of depression.

What you need to do is throw out the suppressed energy. Take five or ten minutes a day, and do gibberish.[38]

Questioner's Comment: Thank you :) Even though it was the only answer, it was the best I could have hoped for.

Q.

If you could ask Santa Claus for a method or a process or a way of handling the stress in your life, what would it look like? For example, meditation has helped me stay calm under stress - but the outer stress is still there.

A.

I have found that meditation helps me to remain more centered, regardless of what is happening outside of me. However, there are situations where the "stress" or the stimulus of the particular environment "takes me over," and I lose my center. For example, if I was on the floor of the NY stock exchange, I would not feel calm. Now this is simply because my meditation is not strong enough. I can only be as aware as I am.

So, in the short term, I might consider removing myself from the really stressful environments, because I do not want to subject myself to this. But in the long term, I need to meditate more deeply, and become stronger in my center. Then I can even go to a casino and not get stressed!

Q.
Please tell me more about Osho. Like the masses, previously I also thought he was an idiot but after reading his books I am totally amazed by this man. He had an art to explain very complex phenomenon in simple understandable words, and he had immense knowledge of psychology, religion, philosophy, meditation etc.

Can someone tell more about his ashram in Pune? If somebody has attended its meditation sessions, please tell me about your experience esp. with dynamic meditation. Thank you!!

A.
I have been a disciple of Osho for 15 years. I am glad you were able to get past the hype and discover this blessed being. As your questions indicate, the best way to get to know Osho is by practicing, over time, one or more of the dozens of meditation techniques he offered.

Dynamic is incredible! The first three stages really get your energy moving, and give you a chance to throw out any garbage you might be holding. The fourth stage is silence, when the grace of Existence simply descends upon you. And finally, you dance, in celebration and gratitude. Beautiful!

Pune -- the ashram is tremendous! A unique combination of many kinds of Western group therapy, dozens of healing modalities, and many, many meditations each day. Truly a special place.

Source: www.osho.com

Q.

How would you define true love?

A.

Most people, when they think of love, think of loving someone or something (a cat). A soft, welling-up from the heart happens, and it is directed towards the beloved.

But the question must be asked: from where did this love arise? It is like a well. In order to get water from the well, the well must be filled from unseen sources.

A person must fill themselves up before they can love others. And for me, the most effective way to do this is to meditate.

Ultimately, (and this is the last step of meditation) you will disappear, and love will arise in your place. You will simply *be* love, radiating the way a flower gives off its fragrance, not caring if there is someone to receive it or not. For me, this is "true love."

11 - Enlightenment

"Slowly, slowly, one has to go on dropping the words and one has to enter into silence. And that is not difficult: once you start moving towards it, it starts happening. The reality is when all words have disappeared, when you are not thinking but you just are...when there is no thought-cloud in the mind but pure awareness, unclouded, an unclouded sky. When there is no thought there is no trembling, no winds are blowing. All is tranquil and quiet. In that quietude one penetrates reality."[39]

--Osho

Q.
Why is enlightenment so difficult when you have to do literally nothing? I'm not sure of the definition of enlightenment but for this question it means a state of pure awareness or no mind no self. So why is it so difficult and why does it take a fair bit of practice? I can only quiet my mind for a short time. But why is it so hard to do!?

A.
The first thing: do not be so concerned about what enlightenment is. Simply do your practice. Watch; be present; be aware; allow what is to be.

The second thing: while it is true that everything you need is here and now, the mind is in the way of noticing. It is like this: on a cloudy night, you cannot see the stars even though you know they are there. The clouds are the mind. The starry night is "here and now." Knowing the stars are there is not the same thing as seeing them, as experiencing them.

Finally, if you notice impatience or frustration, simply be with it. "Hmm, I'm feeling frustrated. Interesting." Accept it from your heart.

Q.

Pls explain (in detail) the meaning of awareness / ultimate consciousness / enlightenment according to BUDDHA. Is nirvana merging with universal / supreme / ultimate consciousness? Does knowing himself mean knowing who he was in past lives?

A.

The only way for you to begin to satisfy your longing to understand these things is to begin to meditate yourself. All of the great masters have said that words are insufficient to describe the truths they are trying to communicate. It is only through *direct experience* that your longing to know will be satisfied. Meditate, and eventually, you will know.

Q.

Do you plan on reaching enlightenment in this lifetime?

A.

I do not plan these things. I simply watch, become aware as possible in each moment, and let nature take its course.

Q. What does the word "enlightenment" mean?

A.

My knowing tells me the word enlightenment has devolved into a multiple-meaning word, like love. "I love my cat." "I love you, sweetheart." "My soul is filled with love for God." Etc.

However, originally, enlightenment referred to a *very* specific state of consciousness. One in which there is a *total,* *permanent* disidentification from the body-mind. One in which the dew-drop of the individual ego and individual soul has disappeared into the ocean of cosmic consciousness.

Enlightenment is *not* satori -- a momentary glimpse of the beyond. Enlightenment is samadhi -- a permanent state.

The word enlightenment does not refer to any particular behavior. It refers to a state of consciousness.

And -- were we to come across a person in this state, it would be difficult to see them, because we don't have the eyes for it. This is why having a master is so important -- and also, it is what makes choosing a master so difficult. "I know I am blind, so it would be useful to choose an enlightened master to help guide me along the way. But how can I choose if I cannot see?"

So we use our hearts and our intuition and we do the best we can and we trust that Existence will guide us to the guide we need.

One last point: judging the behaviors of a truly enlightened one (if we could actually see and know her) is a very tricky business. She is operating from such a height, with such a vast vision, that to judge by our standards is most often missing the point.

To wit: the Zen story of the master who holds up one finger as he talks. A disciple comes, asks a question, and mimics the gesture. The master whips out a knife, and cuts the finger off. KATZ! It is said in this moment the disciple became enlightened.

In modern America, we would arrest the master for assault. But he could see that the moment was ripe. With such a "harsh" gesture, he ended the cycle of birth and death which had been going on for centuries; millennia; and helped the disciple to become free. Cruel or the most loving act imaginable?

Mysterious stuff indeed.

Q.

What is the fastest way to enlightenment? I've done meditation for 35 years, studied the Bible, Baghavad Gita, Koran, Zohar, and others and done Kundalini yoga. And yet, I am still searching for enlightenment.

A.

The answer is in your question. You are still searching for, or desiring enlightenment. And if I understand the masters correctly, enlightenment is the cessation of all desire.

So please, when this question arises inside of you, be intensely present to it. "Ah, there is the mind coming in, wondering when I will get enlightened...interesting." Simply notice the mind desiring.

Then have a cup of tea.

12 - Dialogues

"Bliss is possible only when the mind is no more interfer-
ing, when the mind is no more playing its games, when
you have seen the strategies of the mind, its tricks,
through and through, when you have become aware of
how the mind has been deceiving you for so long."[40]

--Osho

[I have changed the names of the questioners.]

Jim

Q.
What are your thoughts about this: what if the sort of spirituality
experienced by people who practice Buddhism and deep forms of
meditation etc, what they are experiencing is some sort of emanation from, or effect of the Christian God. Generally when I think of
the Christian God, I think that he would be spread out, all throughout nature, everywhere, and maybe when people connect with this
spiritual connectivity usually associated with eastern religions, it's
actually the Christian God?

A.
People who ascend to the heights of meditation (from all traditions,
including Christianity) discard the labels other people use. At the
top of the mountain, it is no longer a Christian God, or a Hindu
God, or even, any God at all. It is simply cosmic consciousness,
undifferentiated, sensed not known, drunk not labeled.

Q.
What do you think about Christianity and cosmic consciousness
achieved through meditation? Do you think one explains the

other? Any chance the feeling of cosmic consciousness is actually some sort of emanation or effect of the Christian God?

A.
I think we connected on another question.

In my opinion, there is no way you will be able to know the answer to your questions until you begin to meditate yourself. Philosophy will not help. Long intellectual discourses on comparative religion will not help. They keep you in the mind.

The answers you are seeking reside *beyond* the mind.

Please -- choose a meditation technique that feels right to you. Begin at the beginning, have patience, and trust that you will be embarking on the greatest journey a human being can take.

Harry

Q.
If everything just is, then how can there ever be any motivation to attain enlightenment? Trying to get enlightenment is a contradiction to everything just being, and trying to even just be in the present is also a contradiction to just being. So why try to attain enlightenment or even just be in the present?

A.
It is true that enlightenment is your "natural" state of being. However, you have forgotten it. You are not aware of it. Your question shows that you are in your mind, thinking about these things. But to become *present* to enlightenment, to become *aware* of your inner core, requires that you go beyond mind.

The stream of thoughts in mind create a screen. The awareness of "who you are" cannot penetrate this screen. Thus, one meditates, so that over time, on its own the mind settles down.

It is like a muddy river. The water in the river is clear. And every-one knows it. And you can sit on the bank and proclaim, with great pride, "I know that the water is clear." But if you look at it, all you see is mud!

However, if the wind calms, and no one steps in the river, eventu-ally the mud will settle, and then we can *experience* the water as clear. This is something like the path to becoming conscious.

One more thing. Yes, the present moment just is, but so long as you are in your mind, you are not aware of it. Take a look at your thoughts. They are either concerned with past or future. The mind is running in this moment, but you are not aware of it. Thus, "who you are" (that is, the witnessing consciousness) is not in the mo-ment. So find a meditation technique that feels right, and give it a try!

Questioner's Comment: Perfect answer. Thanks!

Q.
Who admits to understanding nothing about life? It has been said that true wisdom is realizing you know nothing. Has anyone reached this point? Is it different from enlightenment?

A.
Finding a moment of "don't know" mind is truly helpful. If one is in this state, and one sees a table, one has the possibility of know-ing it as "pieces of wood," or as "many wood molecules." Main-taining "don't know" mind makes it possible for you to grow and expand.

This state of mind is different than enlightenment.

I notice you ask many questions about enlightenment. Please, do not be so concerned with the term. It is like a freshman in physics asking PhD questions about quantum mechanics.

Grow your awareness, and many things will be revealed to you, in their own time.

Questioner's Comment: Great point about a freshman in physics asking PhD questions -- it didn't occur to me that understanding of this subject takes time just like anything else. So is "don't know" mind the same as "beginner's mind?"

A. Yes, it is.

Q.
Meditation vs. life -- Which is more important? If meditation is more important, then would you be willing to meditate for your entire life if it were physically possible to get all nutrition, etc. you needed to survive? Why/why not? If meditation is less important, then why meditate?

If meditation is equally important, then how do you know how to balance meditation time with time for living everyday life? Whatever technique you use, you're making that decision from the perspective of living everyday life, so therefore life is really more important than meditation. So again, why meditate?

A.
Ah, it is my philosopher friend again.

I ask you: would you try to use your arms to lift 2,000 pounds? No -- it is asking your arms to do something which they are not designed to do. You have inside of you a deep longing to touch the Truth. To know it, to feel it, to be nourished by it. But you are asking your mind, through philosophy, to get you there. And it *never* will. You can ask a million questions, read a zillion books, and you will never find the Truth.

(See the chapter on Philosophy for the rest of this answer.)
Questioner's Comment: Makes sense. Thanks!

Randy

Q.
At 48 years old should I give up on my hope to become happy or should I try meditation again? I am extremely lazy and want to become a programmer. But I don't seem to focus. I am thinking of giving up on my hope. I am 48 / single no kids and making $9 / hr in a hotel. PS: I tried Zen Meditation but it does not seems to help.

A.
You are asking many questions in one question.

If you are looking for career motivation, try a self-help book.

If you are looking to understand who you are, if you are seeking to dissolve all suffering in the sense that Buddha talked about it, then by all means go back to meditating. Remember these beautiful words of Rumi:

Come, come, whosoever you are. Wanderer,
worshipper, lover of leaving

Come. This is not a caravan of despair.
It does not matter if you have broken your vows
a thousand times, still

Come, come, and yet again come!

Q.
I am having some concentration, focus, and motivation issues while learning web development. I am starting Zen meditation, and I wonder if it will help me to focus better?

A.
Do not confuse concentration with meditation. Concentration is the focusing of the mind on an object. Meditation is a relaxation; a

gentle witnessing, which brings awareness to what is, and does not use the mind at all -- it watches the mind.

Q.
If I practice Zen meditation for a long time can I develop super powers? Like walking on water, reading the minds of people, and traveling without moving?

A.
Randy -- I have read a few of your questions, and with all due respect, you are heading down a wrong path -- a dark road.

The first thing to be understood is to drop the idea of trying to meditate for anything. If you begin by desiring quieter thoughts or more relaxation or walking on water or concentration or success in your job or any other things you are setting yourself up for failure.

Meditation is the process of becoming aware of what is in this moment. Whatever is, is perfect.

(See Chapter 8 - "Desiring Certain Outcomes" - for the full answer.)

Joe

Q.
How do I explain what's happening to me in meditation? I am new to meditation and lucid dreaming and am trying to learn about how all of it works. I only got into it because I noticed I have an ability that nobody else has. I've always been able to control my energy (since age 12). Now I can send my energy almost on command to wherever I want. But when I do, whichever part I send it to the hair raises on that part.

Anytime you orgasm you get this amazing feeling but now imagine this feeling in every square millimeter of your body. I have only done it three times and it required two things to do it. The first time I was high on cannabis, then experimenting with cough syrup (never did it again and everyone shouldn't do it either) and the 3rd again with cannabis. The second requirement was music.

I can send energy through my hands and feet and thought maybe I could send that excess energy out but I haven't been able to do it since. Can someone please explain this. I am actually looking for a guide to show me what I am ignorant to. I'm sick of getting laughed at when I ask for help on this subject and could really use a lot of help.

A.
Hi. A few questions:

* How old are you?
* Do you do drugs often?
* Do you practice a meditation technique? How many minutes per day?
* What country do you live in?
* What kind of work do you do? (Or are you in school?)

After we take care of a few basics, we can get to your questions.

Q.
Hello. I am 22. I would never refer to a plant that is the reason for everything we have in this world today as a drug but I do smoke cannabis. I practice controlling the energy around me sending it from body part to body part but don't get to do it as often as I like maybe close to 15 to 20 mins everyday or two. I live in the USA and I detail cars. If you would kindly reply as to how you could help me as I don't necessarily trust the Internet especially when you ask if I use drugs. Thank you.

A.

I can reply to a few of your questions. I think ultimately the best thing is for you to find a group of meditators nearby, so you can work with the things you are discovering with others.

The first thing: while I do not have a negative judgment about cannabis, I will say that it adds a layer of complexity to an important process called "discernment." Discernment is the ability of the meditator to "decode" or "decipher" what is happening inside of the body-mind.

An example: as I am meditating, perhaps I see a flash of light. I need to ask myself: was it a reflection from a prism which is hanging in my window? Did a car drive by, sending sun-beams into my room, and across my closed eyes? Or did something internal happen?

If I am high on cannabis, there is a bunch of mental activity happening aside from the usual. Therefore, it becomes more difficult to discern what is what in the inner world. Even without cannabis, discernment is *very* tricky!

I am not suggesting your experiences with energy are imagined or drug-induced. Rather, I am suggesting my sense is you need to get back to basics, as far as meditation is concerned. This means finding a traditional meditation technique that feels right to you, and practicing every day.

Pythagoras, who you might remember from math class, was also a teacher of meditation. He taught the three Ps: preparation, purification, and perfection. Preparation involves a psychological and intellectual study of the subjects which connect to meditation. Purification involves clearing out the body of all of the things which will hinder the meditator. At the appropriate time, this includes changing the diet, drinking lots of water, doing certain kinds of exercises, and yes, stopping alcohol and drugs of all kinds. But purification happens down the road -- no worries!

So, Joe. What do you think? Have I overwhelmed you? Are there are groups nearby which meditate? Did anything I say resonate with you? Piss you off? What would you suggest for next steps?

Q.
What you have said will help me see things through easier but my main concern is finding out how to access that incredible surge of energy. I really think that if I can do it on a normal scale then I can start practicing moving the energy around myself and hopefully manipulate it to use it as a sort of boost. The drug simply assists me with keeping my mind "in the zone" so that simple thoughts or interruptions don't get in the way of what I am doing. I use meditation to help my focus but I think I really might have something different going on.

Regardless of drug use I can simply move my energy on command to where ever I want it to go. I can't find anyone who can manipulate their energy to different parts of the body and show individual reactions for where each part is being energized.

One more question. Why do I get really cold whenever I give out information about life and how things work. Even in a warm room with a heater I still get shivers and that cold sensation. If I talk about government agendas, meditation, aliens, dreaming, etc.

A.
A few things:

I hate to burst your bubble, but many, many people have experienced things similar to (and even more extreme than) what you describe. For one tame example, have a look through this web site:

http://www.chienergyheals.com/

I don't understand what you mean by "a boost." Why do you need a boost?

I understand you can't find anyone who has had similar experiences. I spent ten years with 100 people who did have such experiences. This is why I am suggesting you find a school of meditation, tai chi, chi gung, yoga, or some such practice. You don't have to go through this alone.

The thing you need to see is that the various effects of chi energy moving through the body are side effects of spirituality. For reasons that passeth understanding, you have a certain chi energy manifestation in your body at a young age. That is good and fine and no problem.

But it is time for you to learn to put it into perspective. Jack Kornfield, a meditation teacher, once wrote that siddhas (such experiences) are the booby prizes of spirituality. Yes, such things happen as chi energy starts to move. But so what? Your blood flows all day, your heart pumps, your lymph fluid moves. So what?

What impact does it have on your life? Are you a more compassionate person? Is there more love in your life? More silence? More bliss?

Meditation builds energy, and when one has more energy, it is easier to be heartful, to be conscious, to be concerned and caring about the people around you. This is the purpose of energy and meditation: to become more spiritual, more loving. Moving energy from your thumb to your toe, so that you can feel special or impress your friends, doesn't really get you very far.

One way of caring for people, when you are ready, is doing healing work. I saw a guy from China who did an energy mantra over a glass of water in order to purify it. When you drank the water, you could feel the health and well being from the water entering your

body. Using energy to heal others (as in the practice of Reiki --
google the word) is a blessing, but it takes years of preparation and
purification, through meditation and practice, to get ready for it.

You ask about the cold shivers. There is an old saying: those who
talk, don't know; those who know, don't talk. You have stumbled
upon a certain knowing about chi energy: it might be wise, in most
cases, to keep it to yourself.

Look in your local newspaper, and at the cork board at your local
health food store. Find a class that feels welcoming. Start practicing. Please.

13 - Miscellaneous

"Living on this earth has never been easy. The Buddha famously taught that 'life is suffering,' and that the way out was to get enlightened. That alone was challenging.

"But the Buddha lived 2,500 years ago... before email, cell phones, airplanes, television, computers, global terrorism, environmental disasters, economic recessions, and the expectation that you be a 'peak performer,' a 'super-mom' or just plain 'super.'

"Now it's a whole new story — not only do we suffer, get sick, and die, like other humans throughout history—but we're doing so in a world that's seriously out of whack. We face stresses and demands—despite our amazing comforts and opportunities—that the Buddha never dreamed of, beyond our age-old human condition."[41]

Q.
Does 'meditation music' really aid in being happier? In psychology class my neighbor was listening to meditation music. When I asked why in a polite fashion, she said it made her more relaxed and helped her with her depression by "pushing out the depression." Is this true?

A.
Yes. There are certain kinds of music which bring beautiful energy to the listener. In some instances, it can even shift the mood of the person, or help to dissolve "negative" energy.

For a taste, try the music of Miten and Premal.

Q.
How does a spiritual fasting work? I have been really stressed out lately. I suffer from anxiety and OCD. I have been a little ill and

super stressed out due to personal issues, anxiety, being a mommy, Navy wife, and working full time and still trying to make a career change.

I meditated for the first time and as I was meditating the thought of going through a seven day spiritual fast came to mind. I don't know why. I have never thought about that before. Maybe God wants me to? I don't know. I have always considered myself Christian although I have not been loyal or practiced much.

Anyway...I was really interested in fasting and the best and healthiest way of fasting.

A.
Hi. It is good you are becoming interested in meditation.

To go from where you are directly into a seven day fast, in my opinion, would be quite a shock to the system.

Before you begin making any changes to your diet, I would suggest spending a few months getting into a regular routine with your meditation. If you are like most people, things will begin to happen on their own.

And don't pay too much attention to so-called "messages" that come. This is just the mind talking to you, like it always does. Your job as the meditator is simply to watch, as the parade of thoughts and feelings moves through you.

As you get more proficient at meditating, you will become more aware of the endless stream of thoughts. You may be surprised at all the wild things going on in your brain! Don't get alarmed. We all have the same stuff in there!

Q.
Why do religions need to respond to outside threats?

A.

It seems to me every authentic religion needs to respond to outside threats. From Socrates to the Early Christians; from al Monsoor in the Middle East, to the Mormons here in America, those who bring light to a dark world are persecuted.

Why? Perhaps an analogy is best. If a person is sleeping in a dark room, and then they open their eyes (still in darkness), and then the light is turned on, the first sensation is unpleasant. One is "blinded by the light," and it actually hurts the eyes for a moment.

When a person sits in front of a Buddha, their entire body-mind is being penetrated by the light of the illuminated one. And it can hurt at times. Many people do not want to feel this, so they react in anger. Thus arises the persecution of the Enlightened Ones and their fellow travelers.

Q.

Is Gandhi's message of non-violence and peaceful resistance still relevant today?

A.

Yes. The traditional definition of non-violence may best be provided by Jesus in Matthew 5: "That ye resist not evil: but whosoever shall smite thee on thy right cheek, turn to him the other also." Common translation: "turn the other cheek."

Both Mahatma Gandhi and Martin Luther King Jr. implemented this approach to non-violence in grand fashion, assembling large gatherings of people in parades and marches, which were greeted by police violence. When this violence came, they did not respond violently, and many were injured. The Dalai Lama in Tibet offers another example. When his temples were being overrun by the Chinese army, he chose to flee rather than fight to preserve them.

But there is another approach to the concept of non-violence. This approach comes from the martial art Aikido, as I was taught it. I learned that each person has a right to a sacred space around their body. If someone goes to punch you, you have a right to prevent them from hurting you.

Aikido teaches you to meet an incoming attack with enough force to redirect and neutralize the attack, doing the least amount of damage to yourself, those around you, and the attacker as well. This takes tremendous skill, practice, and awareness.

How does this differ from the "turn the other cheek" approach to non-violence? If we apply Jesus' philosophy, and the attacker hits us twice, we are allowing violence to occur: to ourselves! Is this truly non-violent?

In the Aiki example, we are meeting forceful energy with forceful energy, and if it is done skillfully, *no-one* will be injured. One will dissolve the violent energy before it has a chance to create pain.

Every time I see violence, two images flash through my mind: the Dalai Lama and the Aikido master. It is difficult for me to know whose is the most appropriate response for any given situation.

There is another window into non-violence. One of the effects of meditation is one begins to become disidentified from one's thoughts, feelings, and physical sensations. As awareness becomes stronger, one sees that one is not the mind, not the emotions, and not the body.

If this is true (and I am not asking you to take my word for it -- you can only discover the truth of this statement by meditating your-self!) then the various thoughts, positions, opinions and so forth that you hold will become more fluid. After you have meditated for a while, it is much harder to hold onto a particular mental position, because you see that "you" do not own your thoughts, and in fact, "you" did not even think of the thoughts.

One of the main contributors to conflict in a community is the clash of ideas. One group thinks we should spend money on guns, another on butter. One group thinks we should build a two lane highway, one group thinks it should stay one lane. However, if we are meditating, our attachment to our opinions loosens, and we are able to truly listen to others more deeply and more openly. It therefore becomes easier to collaborate on finding solutions that work for everyone.

There is another point. When people sit together and meditate, there is an incredible "heart-melting" that happens. One feels love and connectedness with people, even if one has never spoken a word to them. At this point, it is much harder to hurt them.

One final angle on violence. Why do people commit violent acts? While this is a complex question, I would say the bottom line is this: if one is wounded in some way, and one is not present to the wound, or is unconscious of the wound, the wound may be expressed through an act of violence.

If this is the case, then violence leads to more violence because violence causes wounds. Then the newly wounded person is more likely to be violent. I have a simple phrase to describe the phenomena:

War creates wounds, and wounds create war.

Q.
Who is Osho (Bhagwan Shree Rajneesh)? Is Osho a cult leader and sex-guru?[42]

A.

It is good that, after you have read his wiki, you still ask about him. Osho was an enlightened master. His main work was to give his disciples various meditation techniques which would help them become more aware of who they are. Do not believe what others say about him: good or bad. Find out for yourself. The best way to get to know him is by choosing a meditation technique which he offered, and giving it a go!

Q.
Was Osho poisoned?

A.
There are many who speculate that Osho was poisoned by the authorities while he was in jail in the U.S. in 1985. They say there is proof that thallium was found in his blood. He died in 1990.

Q.
"Osho. Never born, never died. Only visited this planet earth between Dec 11 1931 – Jan 19 1990." What is the meaning of the sentence used to honor Osho? If he visited the planet earth then why is he said to be dead?

A.
The sentence was actually written by Osho, to be put on his tombstone. It refers to the eternal nature of Being, which lives on both before and after the life of any one physical body. He left his body in 1990. His Being has merged with cosmic consciousness, and lives on.

14 - Although You Didn't Ask

*"Be yourself, just yourself, simply yourself. And remem-
ber, you are taking a great risk when you declare that you
are simply yourself. You don't belong to any crowd, any
herd. These are all herds: Hindus, Mohammedans,
Christians, communists. You are declaring yourself an
individual, knowing perfectly well that it is risky. The
crowd may not forgive you at all. But it is so beautiful to
take the risk, to move on the razor's edge where every step
is dangerous. The more dangerously you live, the more
you live."*[43]

--Osho

Beyond Information

In a world awash with data, please remember: there is something
immensely valuable beyond information. A beautiful, divine silence exists beyond the mind-stuff.

There is a miraculous, subtle force in play which moves us gently
toward this silence. This is the story of how this force worked on
me.

In my twenties, I was steeped in the intellectual world. I was reading spiritual texts, but they did not penetrate. When I turned
twenty nine, I moved to a suburb of the city in which I was living.
This move lessoned to a large degree the noise and distraction to
which I was subjected. In astrological terms, I was in my Saturn
return, so the miraculous force had the stars on its side.

One night, at a dinner party, I exchanged a few words with a new
acquaintance. She mentioned she spent six months in the U.S. and
six months in India. I didn't think much of it.

A few weeks later, I was standing in line at a cafe, and I caught sight of a group of four people laughing and enjoying. Upon looking more closely, I noticed the woman I had met at the dinner party. I was wearing a tee-shirt with the logo of a theatre company with which I had worked. My acquaintance said, "I didn't know you worked in theatre. This man is a world-renowned theatre artist from Germany." Introductions were made, and I sat down with them to have a coffee.

Two minutes later, I was crying my eyes out.

I have no recollection of what transpired between the introduction and the crying. However, I do remember, after I finally calmed down, the German artist saying, "You are ready."

There is an ancient saying. The student does not find the Master; the Master finds the student. In this case, the Master used one of his disciples to find me. A few weeks later, I was immersed in a Zen Theatre course, which combined theatre exercises with meditation techniques.

Shortly thereafter, I became the disciple of an enlightened Master, and began to learn the methods which helped me to have a glimpse of that which lies beyond the spoken word, beyond the zippy thoughts, beyond the emotions, and beyond the sensations of the physical body.

It only took one glimpse of this peace, this silence, this blissfulness, to know that in the end, this is all I need.

Resolving Intractable Conflicts: An Inner Approach

A conflict arises when one or more parties want to change the status quo. If all parties are satisfied with the way things are, no conflict arises. The scope of a conflict can be defined as the difference between the current state of affairs and the desired state of affairs.

An example: "I want to paint my house purple, but I cannot because my neighborhood council's bylaws forbid it." If I would be content with a white house, which in our example would be allowed by the bylaws, there would be no conflict. Conversely, if there were no bylaws relevant to paint color, I could paint my house purple with no problem.

One of the first rules of conflict resolution is that in order to non-violently reach a solution (that is, in order to find a new state of affairs with which all parties feel satisfied), the parties need a safe space within which to meet and interact. In our example, if the house-owner was so angry that he was breaking into the council's offices and smashing the computers, and the council members were stealing the house-owner's stuff and sabotaging his car, it would be very difficult to create a safe space for negotiation.

And yet, on the world stage, this is often how various peace processes unfold. On the ground violence is happening while in the conference room a small group of people is meeting to discuss peace. Have the parties truly created a safe space? Does a tiny oasis in the midst of a sea of violence feel safe?

If there exist two entrenched parties, each bent on getting all of what they want, then violence will continue until the discomfort of the violence becomes strong enough to encourage people to negotiate in good faith. Another example: If Team A wants a given land mass to be governed under Religion A laws, and Team B wants the same land mass to be governed under Religion B laws, we might be in for a long conflict for the simple reason that religious beliefs are so ingrained that to change them is more painful, in some cases, than the worst physical torture imaginable. "Kill the children, burn down the homes and fields, pull out my fingernails, but

I will not allow you to impose your religious rules on me or my township."

Once the opposing parties decide they wish to seek a non-violent resolution of their differences, there exist many techniques and methods which can be employed to find solutions, even in very complex situations. (Richard Holbrooke's book, "To End a War," about the Bosnian peace process, provides excellent examples.)

But how to get to this point? How to get the two or more warring parties to choose good-faith negotiation over violence? Holbrooke offered one answer to this vexing question. He argued that the United States should threaten to send its army to Bosnia if the violence continued. Two teen-age boys are fighting, and the father comes along and says, "Cut it out or I'll give you both a good whipping." While this approach has pros and cons, and may or may not work in the medium and long term, it presupposes the existence of a force sufficiently large to overwhelm both opponents. This approach also requires the political and financial will needed to employ it.

There is another approach. It is admittedly more subtle, and will require time and patience to bear fruit. In my exploration of the inner world, I have found that all dark roads lead to the same place: the fear of death. I can begin in my mind, thinking at length about philosophy or religion or art. I can explore various desires: for money, power, prestige, women. I can delve deeper into the realms of dark emotion: anger, aggression, jealousy, hatred, greed.

But if I keep going; if I keep asking myself, "What is underneath this thought? What is underneath this feeling? Why do I hold onto this philosophical position? Why do I feel greed?" ultimately I get to the same answer: "Because I am afraid of dying."

The root blackness inside of me is the fear of death. Put another way, the root blackness inside of me is the desire for life. (The

Buddha taught that desire is the root-cause of all suffering, and for me, the root of all desires is the desire for life.)

(One caveat here: the blackness is the *desire* for life, not life itself. Life is a well-spring of delight; a fresh river running through a misty forest. It is the *desire* for life, the clinging to life, which creates suffering.)

I am fortunate because I have discovered meditation. And for a variety of reasons, the clod of stuckness inside of me I label "fear of death" has been partially dissolved. It is not as strong as it used to be. For this reason, I feel much more freedom in my life: I feel I have many more choices in many dimensions. I am happier, and I find I can get along with just about anybody. I hold very few intellectual ideas for which I am willing to fight. The light of awareness has partially melted the fear of death, and I have become more peaceful.

It is in the candle's very nature to extinguish darkness. If you bring a candle into a dark room, the room will light up — the darkness will vanish. If you have a rusty pipe, and you run scalding water through it, eventually some of the rust will loosen, and the inside of the pipe will become cleaner. It is the nature of running water to cleanse.

If a person is filled with unconsciousness (greed, hatred, rage, aggression) and the person is greeted with consciousness, awareness, light, and love, eventually the hatred will dissolve. Eventually the behavior of the unconscious person will shift. The beliefs he once held so dear will begin to loosen. The bargaining positions he once was so attached to will become more fluid. Slowly, slowly, more options will begin to appear on the negotiating table.

Does this mean when you sit across the table from Adolf Hitler, you appease him? No. What is needed is fewer leaders who are mired in the thick, black filth which Hitler was stuck in.

.

So the question becomes: how do we seduce people into the process of becoming more conscious? More light? More flexible? More loving? More sharing? More collaborative? How do we seduce people into participating in the variety of activities that are now available to us which deepen meditation and right prayer?

To begin with, I will offer one answer to my own question: those of us who practice need to enjoy ourselves. People want to be around people who are happy, celebrating each moment, smiling, enjoying. Joy, when it is not forced, when it arises from a true place inside, is infectious and magnetic.

Following "My" Bliss?

James Hillman, a well-known Jungian psychologist, has said that a person comes to the earth "knowing" what he is to do here. Joseph Campbell echoes this sentiment when he talks about "following your bliss" (for to do so implies your "bliss" exists inside of you).

The model of the archetypes (that each of us tends to be more of a king, a warrior, a lover, an artist, a businessman) sheds more light on this concept. In my own life, it seemed to me early on that I was here to be an artist.

The interesting thing about meditation, yoga, tai chi, right prayer and the like, is *anyone* on any life path can engage in these activities, with more or less the same effect. The result is that a loosening happens. I discussed this loosening above with regards to ideas, beliefs and bargaining positions. But the loosening also happens around so-called "soul-purpose." If a person starts out on a warrior's life path, meditation can eventually lead him in another direction.

I experienced it as a lifting up. Imagine my artist's life is depicted as a bicycle moving along on a road. When I began meditating, it was as if I began to become detached from the bicycle, and started to float above it. The bicycle still had momentum: it continued along its artist's way. But "I" was free from the path. I could make other choices in my life. And I did. Slowly, slowly, the bicycle lost its momentum, because I had stopped pedaling. And then I had many more options in my life.

It is precisely this state (the state of having many options) which is useful to resolving intractable conflicts.

If we assume that each of us is merrily strolling along on our life paths, following our bliss, what is needed for an individual to decide to meditate? My master has suggested three conditions are needed (kudos to my friend and fellow traveler for sharing these with me).[44]

First, a person must understand that s/he is going to die. Not just mentally, but in a deep way. The moment one really grocks this fact, the big questions arise: Why am I here? Who am I? What is the purpose of life? And the various spiritual practices are known to offer doorways into these questions.

Second, a person must come to know that the endless stream of projects and purposes which the mind creates will ultimately lead nowhere. With the multitude of projects available to us (from home improvements to making our own YouTube videos) this is a difficult thing to see. And yet, I know from my own experience it is true.

To find out, ask yourself: what am I hoping to gain by completing the projects I am working on? Certainly you need a small income for the basics. But beyond this, what is the underlying goal? If you are like me, the goal will have an inner component: I want to be happy, to be content, to feel good about myself.

If you keep looking, eventually you will see that doing the outer-world thing does not deliver the goods. (Don't take my word for it! Have a look inside…)

I spent a long time looking for the most meaningful career for myself. I chose music composition. After a performance of one of my works, sitting exhausted in a cafe, I suddenly realized that no matter how many pieces I wrote; no matter how many awards I won; no matter how many people came to see my extravaganzas; I was still going to have this hole inside of me. I was still going to be miserable.

This is the insight that is needed.

The Buddha said there exists suffering. And — desire is the root cause of suffering. A corollary to these words is, no amount of trying to fulfill desire (and that, in the end, is what "doing projects" is about) will alleviate the suffering. The way is in.

Once I saw that composing wasn't going to reach the core of my wounds, I looked for a deeper solution. This search led me to spiritual discipline.

The third thing that is needed for a person to discover a practice is a person needs to begin to learn from his mistakes. My master used to say, as I remember it, make as many mistakes as you like, but only make each one once.

The great thing about this simple guideline is it leads a person into many different life choices. And as a person explores all the outer world has to offer, living as intensely and joyously as possible, she will eventually discover the truth of axiom number two: nothing in the outer world, ultimately, is going to help. (An aside: it might take a bit of introspection to notice that one is, in fact, repeating one's mistakes.)

We now have more information to guide us in our quest toward spiritual practice. We can remember, in a deep way, that death awaits us. We can attempt to stop duplicating our mistakes. We can examine the deep purpose of each activity we undertake. We can say no when the TV invites us to watch another episode of "My Favorite Show," and instead give our loved one a long, heart-full hug. (I slipped the last one in there without preparation!)

And then, we can spend a few moments in the "Spiritual" section of the book store or newspaper calendar, and see what phrase catches our eye, whispering gently, come, come...As Rumi put it:

"Walk out into the indications of where you must go."

Once the men and women with power and money begin down this path, we all will begin to create a heaven on earth, free from intractable conflict addressed violently.

The Bridge

Two shores;
Separated by a roily river
and eons of distrust.

"I can become a Bridge,"
offers a pile of wood.

For decades, centuries,
cries of "NO" resound
through the hate-filled skies.

Then, at last,
a full moon to the East,
a glorious sunset to the West,
they agree to build.

The wood forms into the Bridge,
and a young girl sprightly walks
across, carrying a bouquet of flowers.

A boy, singing a happy song in
an impish soprano, meanders
along the other way, holding a
basket of fruit.

The mistrust begins to melt:
everyone loves the Bridge.
— — —
The sky clouds over;
the moon becomes new.

Driving west to east,
a truck filled with soldiers;
east to west,
a car laden with bombs.

The violence escalates;
everyone blames the Bridge.

One night, the men from the east
stealthily plant explosives
on their shore's foundation

even as the west men do the same
on their side.

And at the stroke of midnight
(for what better time to do the deed)
they blow the Bridge to smithereens.

A well-meaning pile of wood,
turned to ashes.

The moral of the parable:
While it may be an easy scapegoat
(perhaps because of its silence),
the bridge is neutral:
it is people who decide
what to drive across it –
guns or butter,
flowers or bombs.

On Rag-dolls and Zombies

"Please: No violent video games."

A simple request of a sixth grade computer class in which I was the substitute teacher.

Of course, this becomes "the line in the sand." Thoughts race through the students' minds: "How much can we get away with — our guy being a new substitute and all." "Dude — how do you pronounce your name?" Never mind that I've already veered away from the optional lesson plan which would involve actual teaching and learning.

First there are the sports games. While they provide a comparatively healthy outlet for pent-up energy, they are violent. (Wouldn't you call twenty two big men crashing into each other with all their might violent?) Given the options, the lesser of available evils.

Then there is the otherwise-bright girl who decides to pull up a game which involves throwing rubber balls at a "rag-doll-person," who appears to be injured by the pelting. Certainly violent, but at least she's firing rubber bullets. I could relate to this girl. The peer pressure is intense — fit in or else...

What about the on-screen bicycle rider, careening down a set of stairs, body parts and blood flying. Is this a violent video game? The students I asked did not think so. After all, the only person getting hurt is the bike rider himself.

And of course the zombie games: first person shooters with blood and gore everywhere. The 12-year-old's analysis: "The zombies start out dead, so it's not really violent." I kid you not.

To be fair, one student spent five minutes on a web site which creates opportunities for students from 130 countries to work together on projects which make a meaningful contribution to the health and welfare of the planet. A drop of sanity in a sea of lunacy.

My classroom was being dowsed with violence. Energies from parents, teachers, and friends who are not getting what they want, and who would rather fight with each other than sit down and discuss their differences like grown human beings. Discuss, collaborate, and share the resources we have available to all of us.

Think of the paradise on earth we could co-create if we took all of the resources we employ to beat each other up, and instead used them for the things we all need to live a beautiful and rich life.

I will not be silent any longer. I will speak common sense until my last breath. There is just too much at stake to do otherwise.

Inherited Power

Each human being has the potential to access a wealth of power, manifested in different forms, all ultimately originating from a divine Source.

Before the age of technology, the vast majority of human beings did not have easy access to massive physical, financial, nor spiritual power. With the exception of the children of wealthy aristocracy, and other inheritors of stored power, the average person desirous of power needed to work diligently to amass it. In the process, the person learned about the dangerous consequences of misusing power in any of its forms (recall the Sorcerer's Apprentice).

Today, an average sixteen year old American "earns" the right to maneuver a 2,000 pound vehicle propelled by an internal combustion engine by answering a few simple questions and demonstrating the most basic operating skills. The child is not asked to diagram the life cycle of an oil molecule, to do an environmental impact study on the use of the car, nor to take apart and re-assemble the engine, thus discovering the awesome complexity he or she is about to control.

In this way does modern technology serve as *inherited power* (noted by Michael Crichton and others). The user of modern technology does not need to earn the power which technology provides, nor demonstrate any complete mastery of the tool — the user inherits the intellectual, scientific, industrial, and political power which scores of individuals have collected over the centuries.

There have always been slip ups by the powerful, whether created by carelessness, ignorance, or maliciousness. However, never before have the instruments of power been so mighty, or so widely available to so many.

We as a species must learn a simple lesson, and we must learn it sooner rather than later: actions have consequences, and we are largely unconscious of them. (Chaos theory, a branch of modern mathematics, demonstrates that a butterfly flapping its wings over Hawaii is capable of creating a tornado over Nebraska.)

We are not gods. We are flawed human beings, obscured from the divine by our flesh and blood, but even more so by our limited consciousness. Fear, suppressed anger, and internal scars from a variety of sources make it difficult for us to greet each moment with a loving, appropriate action.

Nevertheless, while there is not much we can do about our status as incarnate beings, we do have available to us many varied tools which can raise our individual and collective consciousness.

Given the fact that we live in a world surrounded by technological devices which translate a simple human gesture into the leveraging of massive amounts of physical (the elevator button), intellectual (the computer keyboard), and energetic (the gas pedal and light switch) power, the need for individuals to engage in consciousness-raising work has changed from a low priority, marginalized idea into an urgent, species-saving concern.

The tools of power already exist in the hands of children, young and old. We must face this fact, and turn to unearthing and passing on wisdom in manifesting this power.

I am not a philosopher. And yet I have a clear sense of what I want for myself and my fellow human beings.

I want us to be able to let the muse flow through our bodies and minds, spirit blending with flesh to create moments of life. Moments filled with the sound of singing; moments frozen in clay or stone; moments when pairs of eyes meet, creating light where no light was visible before.

Each one of us can live a life co-creating such moments. I simply know this is true. It is our duty as human beings alive during an extraordinary period of history to remind each other, in language appropriate to the listener, that to live such a life is within our grasp, and that the tools exist to aid us in reaching for it in our own unique way. Then we may step aside and watch as the moments blissfully ignite.

formlessness

formlessness.
light and darkness.
the forms begin to emerge.
sex. voo doo. money. the arts. food.
creative expression. happiness and sadness.
intellectual thought. romantic love. the assertion
of the will of "i am." the softness of the heart. ahh.
a noticing begins. an observation. a suspicion
i am not any of the forms. i meditate. the
inner shifts: a melting. what remains?
fear of death; clinging to life. KATZ!
dissolving happens. no words.
formlessness.

C2C

Cradle to Cradle Design:
An Essential Perspective as We Begin to
Technologically Enter God's Inner Temple

We are at a tremendously exciting threshold of human development. As a species we have loved, since the time we lived in caves, to "build a better mousetrap." The discovery of fire, the invention of the wheel, and a host of other innovations mark watershed moments in our ability to impact the world around us and improve our quality of life.

However, never before have our new technologies placed us at the door step of God's inner sanctum. When we accelerate particles to the speed of light, crack the human genome, genetically modify plants and animals, engineer things so small it is beyond imagination, and generate enormous amounts of both high- and low-frequency electromagnetic radiation (think cell phones and sonar), we are tampering with the most delicate stuff of Existence.

Up until now, most industrial and product design employed the "cradle to grave" design modality. You gather up some materials, put them together into an end product, use the product until it breaks, and throw it out. You don't pay much attention to how much energy you use to create the product, whether or not the catalysts and intermediate chemicals are toxic, and so forth. This is more or less how a three-year-old functions in the world: with no regard to his effect on his surroundings. And given the fact we have only been creating technology on a large scale for roughly 200 years (fire and the wheel notwithstanding), we truly are children in this game.

However, because of the deep impact of our technology on the world today, it is imperative we become adult-technology-makers, and do so quickly. A company called MBDC has defined and articulated a scientifically rigorous process called "cradle to cradle" design. Rather than attempt to describe it here, I provide their web address:

http://www.mbdc.com/

(For the bulk of the essay, I will assume you have spent a bit of time and energy perusing the MBDC web site. In my opinion, it is time well spent.)

I would suggest it is time for all of our technology, but particularly those technologies which place us at the threshold of God's inner sanctum, to begin the somewhat costly move toward C2C design. As I stated above, it is time that we become tech-adults, and move into version 2.0 of technology development. What does this mean? To begin with, if you make something, be sure you first do no harm. Another basic axiom: be sure you know how to clean up after yourself.

If one makes a plastic container that doesn't biodegrade, the worst that will happen is we end up with a beach-full of dirty plastic. One is working here at a macro-molecular level. The dirty beach is not a great thing, but it is likely not planet-threatening. However, if you deploy a network of low-frequency sonar devices under the Earth's oceans, and it turns out that the sonar waves interact in a negative way with the bioelectrical fields of various animal and plant life forms, then you've made a big boo-boo. Wipe out a strata of organisms, factor in food-chain ecology, and pretty soon we humans do not have anything to eat.

Do we have the consciousness to be working in these depths, at these heights? Have we transformed all of the ambition, hatred, greed, lust, fear, and other darkness inside of us into compassion, patience, wisdom and love? A human who has attained to deep inner awareness, knowing that every gesture creates waves in the universe, when moved to create a new product will be thrilled to know that a process such as C2C design exists to help guide her.

I understand that we are tremendously dependent on our current technologies. I also know that changing over to C2C devices is costly and time-consuming. I am not suggesting that we stop everything, and only deploy C2C technologies tomorrow. However, I am suggesting that each and everyone of us begin to integrate C2C into our lives.

The new technologies, and it bears repeating, penetrate the inner sanctum of God's temple. Genes, quarks, photons, buckyballs, tremendously high (and low) frequencies of electromagnetic radiation — we have, like the sorcerer's apprentice, the tools to force our way into the inner sanctum and muck around a bit. However, do we have the tools to fix what we may break there? Would we notice if we broke something in the first place? Do we have what it takes to move with grace and intelligence there? Is our knowing of grace "grace-full" enough to meet the inner sanctum's standard?

Some argue that others will not use C2C design, and therefore we will fall behind if we take the extra time and energy needed to do so. This, they argue, is especially dangerous with regards to defense technologies. My response is this: I can only be responsible for what I put out into the universe. If someone else makes a big mess, it will be on their karmic tab, not mine. It is all I can do to make sure, in this enormously complex world, that I do not make a major misstep. I believe what goes around comes around: if someone else gets ahead by cutting corners, eventually they will have to pay for the unconsciousness of their actions.

We have enough experience with cradle to grave design (enormous car junk yards, the exportation of huge amounts of waste, and so forth) and incomplete testing of new technologies (Vioxx, asbestos, dioxin, PCBs, saccharin, and silicon breast implants) that we have run out of excuses.

With regards to the defense issue: if I have to create a global toxic waste dump in order to make the tools to protect myself, then what good is this new national security I've bought myself — all I've done is created a really secure mess. It may be that the guy wearing a Kevlar vest, when it stops a bullet aimed at his chest, could not care less about how you are going to dispose of the vest later. But if an ingenious scientist could come up with a new way of making nylon fabric (true story) such that at the end of its life it is possible to break it down into its constituent chemicals, and then reuse the chemicals again, then why not look into doing the same thing with Kevlar?

Again, I am not suggesting we stop making Kevlar vests today. I am suggesting we look into the life cycle of all of our technologies, and begin the move to the C2C design modality as soon as possible.

Perhaps becoming a master of these new technologies also means finding new ways to resolve conflicts. Maybe the price of fighting wars has become so high, on so many levels, that we simply have to grow into the next level of consciousness, where fighting to resolve our differences is not an option, no matter what. Perhaps God will simply not tolerate violence within his innermost shrine.

I see this clarion call to C2C design as a thrilling, positive impulse. It is not about shaming humanity for its past unconsciousness. No — it is about appealing to humankind's highest, most delicate, most intelligent, most beautiful nature. It is about throwing down a gauntlet, issuing a challenge to scientists, businesspeople, engineers, and product designers everywhere: who will step forward and lead us into the remaking of our technological landscape? A landscape we can all feel comfortable calling a heaven on earth.

The Pineal Gland

I had a teacher who once said, "We are all responsible for the dots we connect in our heads." What does this mean?

To me it means that the universe is an infinitely complex and mysterious place. One person could have a brain so large and intelligent that it could contain all of the thoughts and all of the data ever generated by humankind, and still, that person would possess just a drop of water siphoned out of the great ocean of Existence.

Once in possession of all of this data, one may be tempted to form strings of thoughts. To connect data points in order to lead to the formulation of theories to explain things: the weather patterns, the allocation of resources on the planet, the behavior of presidents and paupers, sinners and saints.
My teacher, I believe, was pointing to the notion that stringing dots together may not be as Truth-Enhancing as it looks to be.

At great risk of feeding the intellectual, dot-connecting fire, I offer a necklace of data points, strung together by one of the many portions of my brain. I offer this necklace as an intellectual meeting of the material and the metaphysical, where perhaps the conflicting views of bipolar disorder may interact in a peaceful way.

The focal point of this meeting is the pineal gland. This gland is a small reddish-gray structure that sits near the center of the brain. Western science has shown it is very likely that the pineal gland's activities influence the course of bipolar disease. Both lithium and depakote (valproic acid) have been shown to effect the gland and its workings. Both of these drugs are used to treat bipolar. It is also known that the pineal is light sensitive: its production of melatonin is regulated by the presence or absence of light.

In an article entitled, "The Morning Battleground: Why Bipolar Kids Can't Get Up and Get Going," by Janice Papolos and Demitri F. Papolos, M.D., the doctors write: "All vertebrates possess a pineal gland, and in certain reptiles and birds the gland is situated close enough to the top of the skull to monitor the intensity of sunlight. This "third eye" appears to help animals adjust to changes in the day-light cycles of the yearly seasons. Seventeenth-century philosopher Rene Descartes thought the human pineal to be the seat of the rational soul..."[45]

Manly P. Hall, a theosopher extraordinaire, has penned a work entitled, "The Pineal Gland: The Eye of God."

Here is this little gland, effecting behavior and circadian rhythms through a known biochemical process, and simultaneously referred to as an "eye" and as the seat of the soul. Perhaps the overlap of the physical and the metaphysical can be found within the many occurrences of one word: light.

Light suppresses the activity of the pineal gland, stopping the production of melatonin. Phototherapy (the application of light) is used to treat bipolars and others with sleep disorders. Dawn simulators are used for the same.

Light comes in many frequencies and wavelengths, not just spanning the visible palette of the rainbow, but moving beyond, into the ultraviolet and infrared spectra. (How far into the violets and reds does the seeing of the pineal go? What does television, that chaotic source of light we all know and love, do to the gland in question?)

Light equals energy. Solar cells translate light into electricity. Photosynthesis in plants translates light into chemical energy. When light passes through a car windshield, it slows down, becoming heat energy. Light equals energy, and one form of energy is chi, which martial artists learn to cultivate and preserve and direct. There are those — the breatharians — who say (with certain proof to back their claims) that they live solely on water and sunlight, and have done so for years.

Ah, the mysteries of life.

Perhaps the pineal gland is a key player in the dance of light, no matter what form it takes. Perhaps the "psychotic episodes" which some bipolars experience are in fact "precocious expansions of the eye of God." Perhaps the difficulty that arises during such events has to do with the inability to process, integrate, and ground the varieties of light with which the pineal is being bombarded. Perhaps the person in question is simply a radio receiver which cannot tune to one station, and is receiving cacophonous content from many different signals.

Perhaps in some (not all) cases, the unusual life choices made by folks diagnosed with bipolar are being chosen by a person with (and thank godliness for the gift) an extremely sensitive pineal gland, an "eye of God" open to, and looking for, the Master's wisdom and guidance, even while the spectrum of light is clouded over by the noise of extraneous, non-godly sources of electromagnetic radiation too numerous to list.

Bodhidharma, a great sage of old, spent nine years of his life, day in and day out, sitting in a cave staring at a wall. This was his chosen meditation technique. He was so single-pointed he actually tore off his eye lids to keep from falling asleep. Eventually he became enlightened. What they leave out of the story is what was running through his head during year seven. Or what his sister was saying about him in the village market, as she bought the bread which she left for him at the entrance to his humble abode.

In our world, if he repeated his year-seven thoughts to a therapist, I suspect he would be locked up. A great meditator, a light in this dark world, would be lost. And his sister's pain would be seen as collateral damage resulting from bipolar illness.

I repeat: to me the universe is an infinitely complex and mysterious place. One person could have a brain so large and intelligent that it could contain all of the thoughts and all of the data ever generated by humankind, and still, that person would possess just a drop of water siphoned out of the great ocean of Existence.

I'm prepared to keep to "don't know" mind a little longer, uncomfortable though it may be. Are you?

Ruminations on Serotonin and Endorphins

There is sex. There is bi-polar disorder. There is porn. There is the mystical notion that we are energetic beings, at times filled with juice, and at times running on empty. There is happiness and sadness, love and hate. There is bio-electricity (chi energy) and bio-chemistry (including brain chemistry).

And there is little ole' me, sitting in the midst of this East-meets-West mélange of information, trying to make sense of it all.
The other day I stumbled upon a porn-addition site called Candeo.com. (I am not a porn addict: I am interested in the explosion of porn in our society from an intellectual point of view.) The

doctors there write that porn and other unhealthy sexual activities (i.e., phone sex with strangers) increase serotonin in the brain, thus producing a natural high to which the porn user gets addicted. This is why, they say, it is so difficult to break the porn habit.

Serotonin... serotonin... Wait, I've heard that term. I Google it:

"An indoleamine neurotransmitter, 5-hydroxytryptamine, that is involved in depression, appetite, etc., and is crucial in maintaining a sense of well-being, security, etc."[46]

My memory kicks in. Depression results from, in part, low serotonin levels. In fact, many anti-depressants (God bless psychopharmacology) work by raising the serotonin level in the blood (and by implication, the brain, although technically, there is no way of measuring the actual amount of serotonin in the brain at any given time).[47]

Suddenly, a paradox pops into my mind: there are two methods for increasing serotonin in the brain. One (taking anti-depressants such as Prozac) is judged as responsibly taking care of one's psychological disease. The other (watching porn) is judged as being addicted to a bad thing.

Of course, there are all kinds of moral, ethical, religious, and feminist objections to porn. And, I would argue, there are all kinds of economic, multi-national corporate, and medical objections to taking Prozac. To further complicate things, depression is a complex illness.

But the fact remains: in at least one important way, at the brain chemistry level, both watching porn and taking Prozac has the same effect. The level of serotonin increases.

Suddenly, a new question comes to mind: are there other activities which raise serotonin levels? It turns out there are many studies which show that meditation does so.[48] Acupuncture boosts serotonin levels throughout the body. As a result, it is often used to treat mood issues such as anxiety or depression and to elevate energy levels throughout the body.[49]

There are also many studies which show that qigong (an ancient Chinese form of exercise) increases serotonin and endorphin levels.[50] The following is quoted from a study entitled, "Influences of Wujijinggong on Blood Serotonin and Beta-endorphin Concentrations:"

"The purpose of this study is to measure the endocrine responses caused by 'wujijinggong' training, which is one kind of health-qigong. Blood sample were taken three times, right before and after the qigong training and 30 minutes later. In the trained group the concentrations of noradrenaline, serotonin and beta-endorphin increased significantly. On the other hand, in the untrained group the measured hormone concentrations did not show any significant change. These results suggest that wujijinggong might have an effect on both physical conditions and mentality in the trained."[51]

Meditation, acupuncture, and qigong are all activities which are known to increase the amount of chi energy in the body-mind-Being (within the Eastern world-view). Given this fact, it seems reasonable to postulate a direct correlation between the amount of chi energy and the amount of serotonin in the body at any given moment.

Put another way, the hypothesis is this: consciousness (chi) effects biochemistry.

There is evidence to support this hypothesis. Norman Cousins offered a case study which showed that laughter helped cure Anklyosing Spondylitis, a collagen illness that attacks the connective tissues of the body.[52] There has also been research which shows that psychotherapy (an activity which effects both the emotional and energetic states of being) effects biochemistry.[53]

Winding back around to serotonin, I offer another piece of data to consider: the neurotransmitter is produced in the pineal gland. This gland has long been associated with all things spiritual.

Upon further research, I find a couple of articles which provide a long list of things one can do to boost serotonin and endorphin levels. They include:

* laugh more (echoing back to Mr. Cousins);
* take in the sunlight;
* make love;
* get a massage;
* take St. John's Wort and 5-HTP;
* exercise (the "runner's high" is caused by the release of endorphins);
* eat healthy, high carb meals;
* eat chocolate (good quality, high cacao-content is best);
* eat pineapple, banana, nuts and plums (these foods naturally contain serotonin);
* take B vitamins, folic acid, and vitamin C (they help the neurotransmitters work);
* eat spicy foods like chili peppers.[54]

In conclusion, let us thank the brain chemists for discovering the importance of serotonin and endorphins. And — let us take advantage of all of the natural ways to increase the levels of these vital neurotransmitters.

Have a blissful day!

Synergy

I continue to send out a clarion call for problem solving rather than power tripping; for putting our heads together rather than banging heads; for good-faith collaboration among all merited individuals on any given topic, rather than clever, cunning subversion of the other guy's efforts.

"You're just a dreamer," the pessimists cry. "Our system is built on competition, not collaboration," the realists argue. And yet, all over the world, people get together and solve problems every day. In many cases, everyone wins. One example from 2004:

"Cellular Companies Agree On Multimedia Messaging Standards"

"The nation's cellular companies have agreed on a common standard for multimedia messaging that should enable mobile phone users to exchange photos, video and audio clips just as they do e-mail, regardless of their wireless carrier.

"The technical standards, announced this week, were developed by an industry group...

"[Until now] the lack of interoperability [was] seen as a key stumbling block toward wider usage of each individual carrier's multimedia offerings — and increased wireless data revenues for the companies. ...

"The impact of interoperability was immediate when a common standard was adopted for wireless text messages, better known as short messaging services, or SMS. In less than a year after SMS became interoperable in Australia, monthly usage jumped from about 50 messages per user to 500, according to the research firm Strategy Analytics. In Britain, usage rose from about 50 SMS messages a month to 180 in just six months."[55]

I know there are many other pieces to consider. Agreeing on design criteria. Loss of prior investment. Knowing when to compete and when to collaborate. Agreeing on what is needed or useful in the first place. Freedom of the individual to express his/her own creativity. Unearthing of the best practices, when at times the best creator is not necessarily the most vocal or the best marketer.

As much as I would like to call for simplicity, I can see the complexity of things. And yet, if each individual could bring more heart into each moment, we might find things gelling more easily. The mind tends to quantify, to separate, to segment, to debate. The heart tends to unify, to melt, to know synergy, to love.

As Elton John put it,

"Before you give your love,
there's nothin' more that we can do."

Love-Filled, Precision-Guided Lightning Bolts

Why does my mind
steeped in soot
cause me to cry out,

"War! War! Rage against the vile winds
which rip through the virgin, green fields,
stripping them of their succulent fruit,"

when I know,
from a higher place inside,

"The ultimate weakness of violence is that it is a descending spiral,
begetting the very thing it seeks to destroy. ...

"Returning violence for violence multiplies violence, adding
deeper darkness to a night already devoid of stars. ..."[56]

Where is the Aiki response?
The love-filled, precision-guided lightning bolt
which re-directs and diffuses the in-bound hatred,
leaving only a cool, calm evening bathed
in the light of a crimson sunset.

Do little.
Allow the beyond
to have its way with you.

Disappearing,
only the precious
lingers.

Next Step

There are literally thousands of books, magazines, and websites relating to meditation. My suggestion, which I have made throughout this book, is to find a group which feels "right," and start meditating. Less reading, more non-doing!

In the interim, why not walk into an independent book store, take a title off the shelf which catches your eye, and open to a page in the middle. If what you see speaks to you, then spending time with the book is likely a good next step for you.

Biography

What is essential to say? My name is Prahas. I have worked in the arts, technology, and business. I spent nine years in a school of meditation. I can be reached at foundpra@yahoo.com.

Love.

Citations

[1] Rumi, as quoted by Gabrielle Young at http://www.earthportals.com/Portal_Messenger/gyoung.html

[2] Osho, The Dhammapada: The Way of the Buddha, Vol. 5, Chapter 5

[3] Osho, The Discipline of Transcendence, Vol. 2, Discourse 5

[4] Osho, The Great Challenge, Chapter 1

[5] See Chapter 0.

[6] http://www.news.wisc.edu/13890

[7] See Chapter 0.

[8] Ibid.

[9] Buddha, the "Sutra on Knowing the Better Way to Live Alone" as told by Thich Nhat Hanh in "Old Path White Clouds," as re-printed at http://hunghuuhoang.com/blog/dwelling-in-the-present-moment/

[10] See Chapter 0.

[11] Ibid.

[12] Osho, A Sudden Clash of Thunder, Chapter 2

[13] Eckhart Tolle, http://www.youtube.com/watch?v=ZVLC53Ha658, 55 seconds in.

[14] See Chapter 0.

[15] Ibid.

[16] Ibid.

[17] Ibid.

[18] Coleman Barks, "Unseen Rain," Introduction

[19] Bruce Lee, "Jeet Kune Do," as quoted at http://www.shentaostudio.com/bruce-lee/

[20] http://www.ccel.org/ccel/anonymous2/cloud.html

[21] See Chapter 0.

[22] Sogyal Rinpoche in The Tibetan Book of Living and Dying, HarperCollins, 1993, p. 53.

[23] Shunryu Suzuki, Zen Mind, Beginner's Mind.

[24] See Chapter 0.

[25] Ibid.

[26] Osho, Walking in Zen, Sitting in Zen, Chapter 7

[27] Jack Kornfield, A Path with Heart, p. 44

[28] See Chapter 0.

[29] Ibid.

[30] Ibid.

[31] Helena Petrova Blavatsky, The Voice of the Silence, Fragment III, "The Seven Portals"

[32] Zen Master Seung Sahn Soen-sa, talk given on April 8, 1973, at the Providence Zen Center.

[33] See Chapter 0.
[34] Ibid.
[35] Ibid.
[36] Ibid.
[37] Ibid.
[38] Ibid.
[39] Osho, Let Go!, Chapter 8
[40] Osho, Fingers Pointing to the Moon, Chapter 3.
[41] http://beyondawakeningseries.com/
[42] http://en.wikipedia.org/wiki/Osho_(Bhagwan_Shree_Rajneesh)
[43] Osho, From Death to Deathlessness, Chapter 8.
[44] http://www.shunyo.org/
[45] http://bipolarchild.com/2004/10/vol-18-the-morning-battleground-why-bipolar-kids-cant-get-up-and-get-going/
[46] http://en.wiktionary.org/wiki/serotonin
[47] http://www.ehow.com/how_5615637_measure-serotonin-level.html
[48] http://www.virtualcs.com/meditat/lesson8.html
[49] Citation lost.
[50] http://en.wikipedia.org/wiki/Endorphins
[51] http://www.qigonginstitute.org/main_page/main_page.php
[52] http://www.myhyena.com/2007/09/17/norman-cousins-laughter-best-medicine/
[53] http://www.jsu.edu/criminaljustice/docs/mellen_drugs.pdf
[54] http://www.helium.com/items/977637-natural-ways-to-increase-serotonin-and-endorphins
[55] http://www.crn.com/news/networking/51201557/cellular-companies-agree-on-multimedia-messaging-standards.htm;jsessionid=+kQzpWYVDQOYpWlny12IBw**.ecappj01

[56] Dr. Martin Luther King, Jr.,
http://www.drmartinlutherkingjr.com/mlkquotes.htm

Made in the USA
Charleston, SC
30 July 2013